PLANNING OFFICE SPACES

a practical guide for managers and designers

Juriaan van Meel, Yuri Martens, Hermen Jan van Ree

Review panel: Dr. Francis Duffy, Michael Joroff, Prof. Siri Blakstad

Laurence King Publishing

What do people actually do in an office?

Client BMW Group
Location Munich, Germany
Design Henn Architekten

Client BBC Scotland
Location Glasgow, United Kingdom
Design Graven Images

What types of activities
need to be facilitated
in an office?

What kind of office spaces best support collaborative work?

Client Trust Creative Society
Location Tampere, Finland
Design Trust Creative Society

What kind of
office spaces
best support
individual work?

Client schmidt hammer lassen architects
Location Clemensborg, Denmark
Design schmidt hammer lassen architects

What type of office matches an organization's identity?

Client Selgascano Architects
Location Madrid, Spain
Design Selgascano Architects

What can
make office
spaces really
work?

Client New York Times
Location New York, United States
Design Gensler

Client Caballero Fabriek
Location The Hague, the Netherlands
Design GROUP A

CONTENTS

This publication has
a modest objective –
namely providing a
generic set of office
spaces that can assist
you in creating
successful offices

Client Design Council
Location London, United Kingdom
Design Clive Sall Architecture & Carl Turner Architects

INTRODUCTION

This publication is intended as a practical sourcebook for all those who work on the creation of new work environments, including designers and consultants as well as managers and end-users. In some cases this will involve the design of a completely new office building, sometimes merely the shifting of desks and partitions in existing space.

In any such project, a multitude of decisions have to be taken concerning issues such as floor plans, data-infrastructure, partitions, furniture, finishes, lighting, power-sockets and so on. However, one of the first decisions to be made concerns the office concept. Before rushing into practical details, the client and the design team should have a clear vision of the work environment that needs to be created.

The basic question that has to be addressed is: What type of office space works best? Conventional office rooms or large open-plans? Personal desks or hot desks? A paperless office or one where paper can circulate freely? An office where desk space dominates or an office with coffee bars and break areas? Or perhaps no office at all, enabling people to work on the road, at home or elsewhere?

Finding answers to these questions is far from straightforward. Office space is not just about costs or 'cool' design; it is also about productivity, culture, flexibility and, last but not least, the well-being and happiness of employees. As any office worker knows, seemingly simple design decisions can have a large impact on everyday working life and productivity.

To create the right office environment, it is necessary to look closely at an organization's work processes, identity and ambitions. Different organizations will need different office concepts. Some will be best off with a conventional cellular office, whereas others will flourish in a fully flexible or even virtual office. In any case, the choice should be deliberate and well thought through.

This publication aims to help clients and their design teams to make the right choices by providing them with ideas, inspiration and guidelines. It does not propagate a single office concept or design formula, but offers a neutral overview of the pros and cons of different office concepts and different types of space. Thereby, we hope that the book helps clients and their design teams to think critically and create unique office solutions that really work.

Hermen Jan van Ree, Yuri Martens and Juriaan van Meel

By setting clear and explicit objectives, all stakeholders involved will have similar expectations concerning the new office concept

Client facebook
Location Palo Alto, United States
Design studio o+a

OBJECTIVES

The main purpose of an office building is to support its occupants in performing their tasks and activities, preferably at minimum cost and to maximum satisfaction. Alongside this functional purpose, office buildings have an important social and symbolic function. The design and layout of spaces can, for example, encourage interaction or stimulate creativity. Furthermore, the physical office can convey a strong cultural message to employees and visitors about the organization's identity or brand.

To establish an effective office concept, the underlying objectives should be clear. What benefits should the office deliver? Should the design focus on cost reduction or employee satisfaction? Should it strengthen the existing culture or act as a catalyst for cultural change? Should it focus on facilitating individual work or group processes? And to what extent should the design take the environmental impact into account?

Clear answers to such questions significantly contribute to the success of a project. They provide the framework for decisions to be made during the briefing and design processes. Furthermore, explicit objectives help to communicate design proposals to the employees who actually have to work in the office, explaining why and how changes take place.

Important considerations
- What is the need for a new office concept and what are the benefits aimed for?
- What problems need to be solved (i.e. what is wrong with the present office)?
- How does the new office concept relate to organizational changes and future needs?
- Is the project business or cost-driven?
- Are the objectives and design proposals clearly communicated to the users?

In this chapter we will describe nine objectives that are often associated with new office concepts.

It is important to note that many of these objectives are closely related to one another, but that some of them can also be conflicting. For example, financial objectives aimed at cost cutting might conflict with the desire to increase employee satisfaction.

Furthermore, it is important to realize that the described objectives are still rather broad and open to interpretation. On a project basis they need to become more explicit, specific and detailed. They also need to be prioritized, clearly indicating which objectives are critical and which are not. After all, everybody wants an office that is efficient, flexible, sustainable etc. The question is how these abstract goals should be interpreted and which objectives are more important than others.

Enhance productivity

The most important objective is also the most difficult one: to enhance productivity. The term productivity refers to the fine balance between the total occupancy costs of a workplace and its contribution to employee performance. Basically it is about improving staff output against fewer costs. Although reducing costs is often the prevailing paradigm, there is a growing case for providing an effective work environment to improve employee performance.

To create an environment where employees can be optimally productive, the office should, first of all, meet basic standards concerning ergonomics and indoor climate (thermal comfort, visual comfort, air quality and acoustic comfort). While these so-called 'hygiene factors' do not actually enhance productivity, they will certainly have a negative impact on it if they do not meet basic requirements. Secondly, the work environment should match the activities that need to be carried out. Different work processes tend to require different types of work space. For example, head-down work will call for a relatively distraction-free environment, in which people are not diverted by workplace chatter and telephone calls, while interactive processes may work well in environments that are buzzing with activity.

The exact relationship between the physical work environment and productivity, however, is elusive and complex. Although important, office design is only one of many factors that affect productivity (other factors include work content, colleagues, salary, etc.). Furthermore, productivity is a rather indistinct construct that is notoriously difficult to define in most office-based organizations. For these reasons, productivity enhancement in itself tends to be too abstract an objective for guiding the office design process. In most cases, it is more practical to translate this very general objective into more tangible targets concerning cost, interaction, creativity or satisfaction. These and other objectives will be discussed on the following pages.

Relevant considerations
- To what extent can productivity be defined and measured?
- What are the key factors most likely to enhance productivity?
- How can office design influence these key factors and/or enhance productivity?
- What are the differences between individual, departmental and organizational productivity?

Reduce costs

Cost reduction is a major objective in many projects. Accommodation is expensive and not always utilized as efficiently as it could be. On average, workstations in office buildings are physically occupied only 50 to 60 per cent of the time, while they represent major costs for leasing, cooling, maintaining and cleaning the space needed.

Increasing workplace utilization and office densities can help significantly to trim property costs. Desk sharing reduces the need for workstations and open planning makes it possible to 'squeeze in' more employees. Another measure that helps to save costs is standardizing the size and fitting out of spaces, reducing the costs related to internal moves.

Cost savings should, however, always be seen in relation to employee performance. While the running cost of an office building represents a mere 10 to 20 per cent of total operating expenses, it is still relatively low compared to employee costs. This means that efficient use of space is important; but even more important is creating an environment where people can work effectively.

Another important consideration is the trade-offs between investment costs and running costs. Desk sharing, for example, can significantly lower the running costs of the building, but generally requires higher investments in IT and furniture.

Relevant considerations
- What is the need for cost reduction (and what are the benefits anticipated)?
- What are the options to reduce the floor area per workstation?
- What are the options to increase the utilization of workstations?
- How can the frequency and costs of internal moves be reduced?
- To what extent do cost savings endanger staff satisfaction and productivity?

Increase flexibility

Closely related to cost reduction is the desire to create a flexible office environment. As today's organizations are characterized by frequent changes in both structure and work processes, buildings are ideally able to facilitate these changes when they occur – preferably at minimum cost and with minimum disruption to the business and day-to-day activities.

With regards to flexibility, it is important to determine the type of organizational dynamics a building should be able to accommodate. Are staffing levels subject to strong variations, does the composition of teams change often or is the entire organization likely to significantly change as a result of mergers or subdivisions?

In response to different types of change, varying types of flexibility are required. A distinction can be made between building flexibility (i.e. buildings that can easily be extended, split up and/or sublet), spatial flexibility (i.e. floor plans that can easily be converted from cellular offices into open-plan spaces and vice versa), and workplace flexibility (i.e. workplaces that can be flexibly used by any employee).

An important consideration is the standardization of workstations and room sizes. If the majority of work spaces and meeting spaces have the same size, or at least modular sizes, changes in the physical work environment become cheaper and less disruptive.

Relevant considerations

- To what extent should the building be flexible, extendable or dividable into subunits, providing possibilities for growth or shrinkage of the organization?
- To what extent should the spatial layout be flexible, providing possibilities for various office concepts within the same structure?
- To what extent should workstations be flexible or universal, providing possibilities to move people around with a minimum of technical adjustments?

Encourage interaction

Interaction between employees is seen as a critical success factor for organizational performance. The exchange of information and knowledge not only helps to improve organizational learning and teamwork, but also enhances social cohesion and cross-fertilization. The physical layout of the work environment plays a crucial role in this. Floor plans localize people and can thereby stimulate or hinder interaction.

The ambition to encourage interaction is often translated into open office layouts, literally breaking away the physical and symbolic barriers to communication. Other design solutions are the improvement of adjacencies between groups, the use of transparent partitions and the creation of natural meeting points such as work lounges and coffee bars. All these design interventions generally help to stimulate interaction.

At the same time, it is important to acknowledge that interaction is, obviously, not only affected by spatial layout. Social conduct, behaviour and culture are just as important. Furthermore, it is important to realize that the flip side of stimulating interaction is increased bustle and noise in the office. It is difficult to pin down how this affects employee productivity, but a lack of social and visual privacy can have negative implications for tasks requiring concentration. Different organizations will ask for a different balance between communication and concentration.

Relevant considerations

- What is the main purpose in encouraging interaction (e.g. workplace learning, improved teamwork, enhanced decision-making)?
- What type of interaction should be stimulated (i.e. formal or informal, continuous interaction or chance encounters)?
- Between whom should interaction be improved (i.e. within or across departments, between employees only or also with external parties, such as clients)?
- What is the desired balance between communication and concentration?

Support cultural change

Many organizations spend a great deal of money and energy on rethinking and changing their corporate culture. Changing a culture, however, is one of the most difficult managerial tasks. Culture is by definition deeply rooted and therefore difficult to transform. Office design, however, can be a powerful tool or 'change agent' in this process.

Buildings and their interiors are highly visible, tangible and always present. Therefore, office design may be a more effective tool for cultural change than the usual management speeches and newsletters. Physically locating senior managers and junior employees in the same space, for example, will be much more powerful than simply stating that the organization should be less hierarchical.

Changes in the layout and design of the work environment intended to support cultural change should, however, go hand in hand with changes in management style and working practices. As an organization you need to consider carefully what sort of culture you wish to create and what the real identity of the organization is. It can be counterproductive to create an ultra-modern office if the organization as a whole has a rather conventional mentality.

Relevant considerations
- What type of message should the office convey to both staff and visitors?
- To what extent is that desired message in line with the existing culture?
- How is the new office related to a wider programme of cultural change?
- What are the key words associated with the new office (e.g. dynamic, innovative, sober, cosy, welcoming)?

Stimulate creativity

Creativity is rapidly gaining in importance to both organizational and individual work processes. Many businesses aim to excel through their capacity for continuous innovation, for which creativity is essential. Again, layout and design of the work environment can play a crucial role, creating spaces that stimulate the spontaneous exchange of ideas, or secluded areas for individual thinking.

Generally, creative work is characterized by being both highly cognitive and highly social. Creative workers need a combination of frequent interaction with peers and intense, focused concentration. Such work might require atelier-like open spaces or a mix of individual work spaces and informal meeting spaces. Furthermore, a lot of attention is being given to the routing within offices, aiming to increase chance encounters for enhanced cross-fertilization.

Also the use of shapes, materials and colours tends to get a lot of attention. Some creative organizations opt for highly colourful and diverse design schemes, filled with 'props' such as billiards, juke-boxes or beanbags. Such 'fun' environments may, however, not be relevant to all creative processes or types of organization. Even rather clean or supposedly 'dull' environments, such as laboratories and research spaces, can be creative. What counts most is that the environment is not restrictive, allowing end-users freedom to think and act.

Relevant considerations
- What type of creativity should the office stimulate (i.e. individual creativity or group processes)?
- To what extent should creativity be stimulated (i.e. an entirely creative work environment or a limited number of creative spaces such as brainstorming rooms)?
- To what extent should creativity be supported by 'props' and alternative shapes, materials and colours?

Attract and retain staff

For almost any organization, attracting good quality staff and retaining highly-skilled personnel is critical. This can be done by providing meaningful work, promising career prospects and attractive financial compensation; but the physical work environment can also play an important role. Providing employees with comfortable, attractive surroundings tells them that they are valued by management and helps to make a good impression on job applicants.

In essence, creating an attractive work environment has to do with providing healthy and comfortable workplaces that are well-lit, properly ventilated, sufficiently cooled and ergonomically designed. To keep staff 'happy', however, the more psychological and behavioural needs and wants of employees are also important. Certain employees might attach particular importance to privacy and personal space, whereas others might place more value on, for example, the availability of coffee bars or reading rooms. The freedom to work wherever and whenever also tends to be highly valued by employees.

It is also important to ensure, however, that the demands and wishes of employees do always match those of the organization as a whole. For example, the introduction of desk sharing and open-plan offices initially tends to result in resistance. In such cases, careful attention should be given to the 'trade-offs' for employees. The loss of personal space can be compensated by, for example, more attractive design and high-tech office tools or a greater diversity of work spaces to choose from.

Relevant considerations
* What do employees value in their work and work environment?
* How important is the physical work environment to them?
* What types of work environment are successfully used by competitors?
* When introducing more efficient office concepts, what is the benefit to the employees?

Express the brand

Branding is about creating a particular image or perception of the organization and its products or services among customers or other strategic stakeholders. Traditionally, branding is the responsibility of marketing departments and strongly focused on logos, packaging, websites and advertisements. But, as stated previously, the physical work environment can also be used to convey a particular message or identity, working as a showcase or three-dimensional business card to the outside world.

A common means to brand the office environment is the incorporation of 'brand visuals' (logos, slogans and company colours) in the fit-out of the building. This is a very literal and direct way of branding. In addition, there are also more subtle ways to express a company's brand. For example, a company that wishes to brand itself as very innovative may choose an office concept that is equipped with state-of-the-art technology, funky brainstorming rooms and generous circulation spaces for informal communication.

When looking at branding and office design, it is important to acknowledge that different office areas will ask for different branding expressions. In 'front offices', where visitors are greeted in waiting areas and welcomed into meeting spaces, branding can be explicit and direct, immersing visitors in the company brand. In 'back offices', accessible to employees only, branding may be more tuned and subtle, not providing too much distraction from day-to-day work processes.

Relevant considerations
- Does the organization have an explicit branding strategy?
- Can the new office concept be related to a wider programme of internal and external branding or marketing?
- Should there be a difference between the 'front office' and the 'back office'?
- What message should the office convey to employees and visitors (e.g. integrity and confidentiality, creativity and freedom, etc.)?
- To what extent is that desired branding message in line with the existing identity of the organization?

Reduce environmental impact

Office buildings have a large impact on the environment as they require a lot of raw materials to build and even more natural resources to run. Next to transport and travel, buildings are the largest consumer of energy and therefore a significant contributor to the emission of greenhouse gases. Furthermore, the operation of office buildings requires large amounts of water and leads to a lot of waste.

The choice of office concept – in particular the footprint of workstations and whether or not they are to be shared – has a considerable influence on the environmental impact of an office building. Small footprints and the flexible use of workstations not only leads to a reduction in space requirements, but also need fewer materials and less maintenance, less heating and cooling, less lighting and cleaning and less demolition work at the end of the life cycle.

The flexibility of office space also leaves appreciable scope for environmental savings. If a lot of building work is required each time the organizational structure and / or the work processes change, the environment is negatively impacted. A more open and flexible office can result in less refurbishment work when changes occur. In extreme cases, office buildings may be so flexible that they can also accommodate completely different uses, such as apartments.

Other environmental considerations are more closely related to building design and fit-out. These may include the use of sustainable materials, detailing that requires little maintenance, alternative energy sources and only heating or cooling during core operating hours.

Relevant considerations
- What are the options to reduce the carbon footprint of the office?
- What are the options to reduce the consumption of raw materials?
- What are the options to reduce the consumption of energy and water?
- What are the options to reduce the production of waste?
- What are the options to increase the recycling of energy, water and waste?

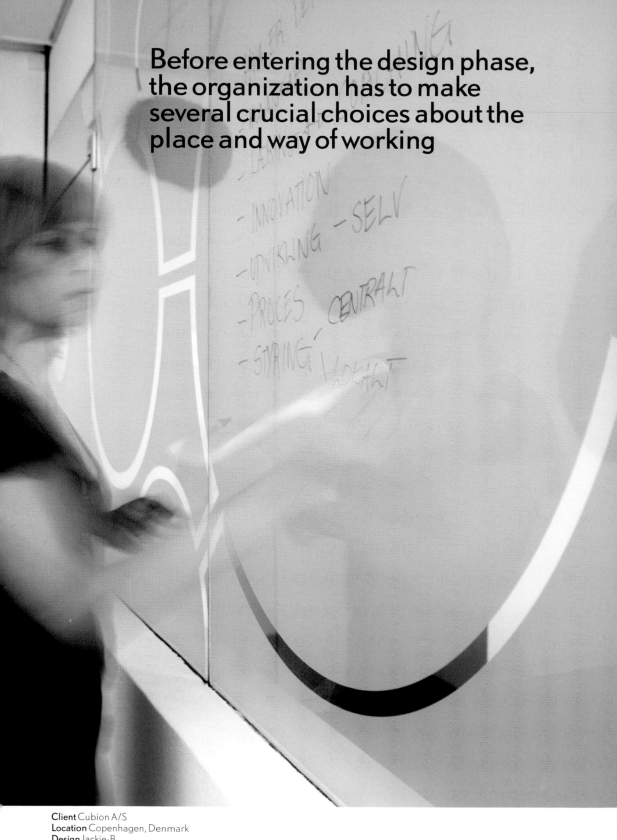

Before entering the design phase, the organization has to make several crucial choices about the place and way of working

Client Cubion A/S
Location Copenhagen, Denmark
Design Jackie-B

CRUCIAL CHOICES

When translating the organizational objectives as described in the previous chapter into a tangible work environment, a number of important decisions have to be made. Where and how do we want to work? What kinds of work space support our activities best? How much do we make use of new technologies? Grouping these and similar questions into categories, there are six critical topics for decision-making.

Location: the office versus elsewhere

Do employees work at the office or do they have the freedom and possibility to work elsewhere, e.g. at home, in clients' offices or in public places such as coffee shops?

Use: allocated workstations versus hot desks

Do employees get their own personal workstation or do they make shared use of various unassigned work spaces?

Layout: with walls versus without walls

Does the office layout primarily consist of open spaces or enclosed rooms? Or does it consist of a more balanced combination of the two?

Appearance: neutral space versus expressive space

Is the office a neutral, primarily practical space to work, or is it an expressive, visually arresting showcase?

Filing: less paper versus paperless

Do employees work in a fully digital work environment or is there room for tangible books and reports?

Standardization: tailor-made solutions versus one concept for all

Does the office concept apply to the organization as a whole or are different departments free to make different choices on the above-mentioned five topics?

These questions are of a strategic nature and have a direct impact on the way an organization functions. For that reason they are typically management decisions. Once these decisions have been taken or endorsed, they can be used to develop a more detailed brief and design for the project. In this chapter each of the six crucial choices are briefly discussed.

Location

Nowadays there are many alternatives to the traditional office building as a place to work. Mobile workers equipped with smart phones or PDAs, who can be spotted all around us, are proof that the virtual office is a reality. At the same time, much of today's business is still very much location-bound. The majority of employees still commute on a daily basis to an office building, spending a lot of time in traffic jams and on overcrowded public transport.

Increasingly, however, employees wish – or even demand – more freedom and flexibility in their time and place of working. Such freedom tends to improve employee satisfaction and individual productivity. At the same time, working away from the office has a negative impact on face-to-face interaction between colleagues. There are fewer opportunities for the proverbial chat in the corridor or at the coffee machine, which is believed to be crucial for knowledge exchange and social cohesion. Furthermore, on-the-spot management needs to be replaced by distance management, which is only possible if a sufficient level of trust exists between managers and employees.

The relevance of mobile working (also referred to as teleworking or e-working) varies from one organization to another and from one type of job to another. Mobile working comes naturally for job types that have always been highly mobile, such as sales representatives, account managers and consultants. However, it may be less practical for traditionally office-bound jobs such as secretaries and managers. Furthermore, personal preferences and individual abilities play an important role. Some people appreciate the freedom and flexibility of working away from the office, while others function best in the company of their colleagues, in an environment that is clearly separated from their private world.

Relevant considerations

- To what extent is everyday face-to-face contact at the office necessary or desirable?
- Is there enough trust between management and employees to allow for mobile working?
- Are managers capable of switching from direct supervision to output-based management?
- Can mobile working help to significantly reduce commuting times to and from the office?
- Are all the necessary technological tools – both hardware and software – available?
- Have steps been taken to ensure suitable working conditions away from the office?

MOBILE WORKING

Advantages	Disadvantages
+ More freedom and flexibility for employees	- Less face-to-face interaction between colleagues
+ Potential increase in individual productivity	- Danger of decrease in group productivity
+ Possibilities to combine work and private life	- Blurring of boundaries between work and private life
+ Less need for costly office space (only when combined with flexible use of space)	- Requires upfront investment in suitable working conditions outside the office and tools to support mobile working
+ Can help to reduce peaks in space utilization	- Requires a high level of trust between managers and employees
+ Can stimulate digital working	
+ Reduction of daily travel to the office	

Use

Workstations are occupied for only a limited amount of the time they are available. Desks and chairs stand empty because their users are attending internal meetings, working at client offices or simply absent due to annual leave. Varying activity patterns and working away from the office both significantly decrease utilization rates. In turn, low utilization rates provide a strong business case for the introduction of a work environment where people use 'hot desks'.

When introducing a flexible work environment, however, it is important to decide just how flexible the office should be. How many workstations need to be realized for any given number of employees? To answer this question, accurate figures about the average utilization, or more safely the peak utilization, of work spaces are useful. Furthermore, it is important to consider the degree of zoning. In its most extreme form, employees are fully 'footloose' within an office building. Most organizations, however, prefer to give departments and/or business units their own particular zone to ensure that employees interact sufficiently with direct colleagues.

Again, the relevance as well as the potential gains of a flexible work environment differ strongly between organizations and job types. Highly mobile employees are not very likely to put much value on having their own personal workstation, especially when benefiting from an attractive and well-equipped work environment. Employees spending most of their working time at the office, however, are most likely to be more reluctant to

give up their 'territory'. In both cases, introducing desk sharing requires a lot of engagement, communication and guidance in order to succeed.

Relevant considerations
* What is the average and peak utilization of workstations (measured over various weeks)?
* How many employees work part-time and to what extent do people work away from the office?
* Are all the necessary facilities – both adjustable furniture and flexible ICT – available?
* How big are the potential savings (taking into account the required upfront investments)?

SHARED USE OF WORKSTATIONS

Advantages	Disadvantages
+ Efficient use of costly office space	- Requires a (largely) paperless way of working
+ Employees can choose between different types of work space for different activities	- Requires a strict clean-desk policy; no possibilities for personalization
+ Employees are more likely to meet different colleagues when they move from one workstation to another	- Danger of a lack of a sense of territory and belonging
+ Can reflect or strengthen a flexible and dynamic business culture	- Danger of a lack of team interaction when employees 'wander' through the building
+ Can enhance digital working	- Danger of queuing for favourite work spaces
	- Minor inefficiencies when moving from one work space to another (logging off/on, adjusting chair and desk)

Layout

The physical fit-out of an office building is an important organizational decision, not least because it will have a significant impact on the way people interact and feel. Open-plan offices, for example, are strongly associated with communication and interaction, but also with noise and a lack of privacy. Cellular offices, on the other hand, imply concentration and confidentiality, but possibly also social isolation.

Obviously, reality is less black and white as open offices can be quiet when everybody has got their heads down working, while enclosed offices hardly provide any peace when shared with a noisy and talkative colleague. Intermediate solutions try to combine the best of both worlds, providing employees with open areas for interaction and study booths for concentration.

Whereas the cellular office has always been popular among employees, the open office is currently the prevalent solution. The underlying rationale is that today's organizations highly value collaboration and teamwork. A more mundane reason lies in the efficiency and flexibility of open offices. They can accommodate more employees, can easily be reconfigured and do not require costly partition walls. In cellular offices, a certain degree of efficiency can be achieved by standardizing room sizes.

The optimal layout solution depends on the activities that need to be facilitated. Office workers with complex tasks that require long periods of uninterrupted concentration are likely to perform best in spaces that provide a certain degree of privacy and quietness. Employees performing routine activities or working in teams can more easily be accommodated in open spaces. Another important factor to take into consideration is culture. Private rooms may reinforce a hierarchical or individualistic culture, while open layouts can be used to underline group values and lateral organizational structures.

Relevant considerations
- What is the desired balance between communication and concentration?
- To what extent is there a need for collaborative settings with frequent interaction?
- To what extent is there a need for confidentiality and/or frequent one-on-one meetings?
- To what extent are privacy and room size considered as status symbols?
- How efficient and flexible does the work environment need to be?

OPEN LAYOUTS

Advantages	Disadvantages
+ Encourage and stimulate interaction	- Danger of noise and interruptions
+ Efficient use of costly office space	- Lack of visual privacy
+ Workstations can easily be reconfigured, without having to move walls and/or partitions	- Danger of overcrowding
+ Can reflect an open and communicative business culture	- No possibilities for individual control of indoor climate (temperature, ventilation)
	- Implementation may meet resistance from employees when they are used to cellular offices

Appearance

Office design is a very visible expression of the culture and identity of an organization. The building's 'look and feel' give visitors a first impression and for employees they have a strong impact on the general work atmosphere. For example, a large open office floor filled with greyish modular workstations will create an image and atmosphere entirely different to a club-like space filled with designer furniture.

It is tempting to state that the expression of offices in general should become more vivid and colourful, since most offices are rather bleak and dull. However, creating a visually stunning office decor is not a goal in itself. Again, one should determine what works best for the organization. In some cases, the expression of the office should just be neutral, utilitarian and little more – for example, when an organization wishes to convey a 'no-nonsense' image, telling clients that their money is not spent on lush office interiors. In other cases, there may be a need for a highly expressive, challenging or even spectacular design to portray an image of uniqueness, telling the world that this is not just another office.

To determine what type of expression is relevant, it is important to make an analysis of the organization's brand and culture. To get inspiration and ideas, it is recommended to visit other projects, to get an idea of what types of design are appealing or not. Using this input, try to formulate the desired expression in a limited number of key words, which may

also indicate certain design challenges – for example, stating that the office should be 'serious and representative, without being boring or formal'. Other ways to communicate the desired expression are reference images and the use of metaphors (e.g. the office as 'club', 'city', 'laboratory', 'factory' or 'campus').

Relevant considerations
+ Can the expression of the office be related to the branding strategy or desired cultural changes of the organization?
+ Do different stakeholders share the same view of what the office should look like or do they have conflicting ideas?
+ Is the desired expression of the office clearly defined (and not too vague or directionless)?
+ To what extent should the expression of the office be controlled and managed? Is there room for input by end-users (e.g. bringing in their own 'props' such as posters, cartoons or plants)?
+ Should there be a difference in the 'look and feel' between areas where employees work and areas where visitors have access?

EXPRESSIVE DESIGN

Advantages	Disadvantages
+ May make the office a more attractive, user-friendly and homely place to work	- Too many visual stimuli (colours, shapes, messages) can be distracting for employees
+ Can help to 'build and live' the company brand	- The 'wow effect' of expressive design may wear off fairly soon after moving in
+ Helps to communicate the uniqueness of the organization in question	- Too fashionable or trendy a design expression may quickly be outdated
+ Spectacular design can generate publicity and attract visitors to the building (and thereby the company)	- Investing large sums of money in designer furniture and 'cool' architecture may not give the right impression to clients and other stakeholders

Filing

In a conventional office building, a great deal of the available space is used for the storage of paper files and documents. When introducing mobile working and/or a flexible work environment, such files and documents can form a major obstacle. Employees cannot work fully 'footloose' when they have to carry piles of paper around. Moreover, paper filing can inhibit knowledge exchange within organizations. Digital information is simply easier to share than information hidden in someone's personal pedestal.

Using increasingly powerful and user-friendly tools for scanning, storing and processing data, organizations are increasingly working digitally. Nevertheless, physical files and documents are persistent. One of the main reasons why people still have a preference for paper is the ease of reading and annotating. Furthermore, hard copy documents can be glanced through from beginning to end without having to scroll down page by page. Advances such as e-books are likely to change this situation rapidly, but for now the establishment of a paperless office still requires a major effort to succeed.

As with the other choices discussed in this chapter, the appropriate degree of digitalization will depend on both prevalent work processes and the culture of the organization. Paperless offices, for example, are very suitable for efficient bureaucracies that work with accurate and standardized data. The corresponding clean desks, however, may be less relevant for organizations or job types where work processes are of a more unpredictable nature. Researchers, journalists or designers are generally good examples of 'pilers' who will be opposed to the rigid introduction of a paperless office or a 'clean desk policy'. On the other hand, 'filers', such as controllers or managers, are likely to show less resistance to a fully digital work style since they are already used to systematic filing.

Relevant considerations
+ What kind of information are employees dealing with and to what extent can this be digitalized?
+ Are all the necessary technological tools available and are employees trained in digital working?
+ How much shelf space is allocated per employee for the storage of frequently used files?
+ Does the current organization primarily consist of 'pilers' or 'filers'?
+ To what extent do strict 'clean desk policies' fit into the organizational culture?

PAPERLESS OFFICE

Advantages	Disadvantages
+ Digital information can be available at all times and places	- Requires upfront investment in hardware, software and training
+ Enables flexible and mobile working	- Requires guidelines and policies for the way people work
+ No need for physical filing space	- Requires a certain level of 'enforcement' by management
+ No danger of confidential or sensitive papers lying around the office	- May contradict with people's natural tendency or desire to read and work on paper
+ Tidy and neat work spaces that can easily be cleaned	

Standardization

For all choices discussed so far, it is important to consider whether they apply to the entire organization or whether different business units can make different choices. Generally, organizations are not homogeneous entities, but a mix of different work streams, people and cultures. For example, a marketing department will be different from an engineering department. The question is how far such differences should be expressed in the office concept.

A major advantage of applying a one-and-the-same concept across the board is the ease of acceptance. For example, the introduction of a flexible work environment will be more readily accepted if this concept applies to every employee in the organization, including top management. Some experts claim that this is the only way to ensure success: implement it company-wide or not at all. The disadvantage of a 'one size fits all' approach is that it easily tends to become too dogmatic, overlooking existing differences between the various departments and/or business units within the organization.

It is important to determine in advance which principles and policies must be complied with and where a certain degree of flexibility and customization can be allowed. With regards to the layout of an office, for example, it is beneficial to standardize the size of spaces and the position of partitions, while the exact use of these spaces can easily be left to the different departments. One department might use enclosed office spaces to create extra study booths, while another may use the same spaces to create their much-desired small meeting rooms. And so, while the overall concept and flexibility is preserved, individual departments can still influence the design of their work environment.

Relevant considerations
- How much difference in culture is there between the various departments and/or business units?
- Are most work processes similar throughout the organization or do extensive differences exist?
- How important is it for the organization as a whole to project a clear and consistent image?
- What kind of decision-making culture exists within the organization (central or decentralized)?

ONE CONCEPT FOR ALL

Advantages	Disadvantages
+ Clearer, easier to 'sell'	- Danger of becoming too dogmatic
+ More flexible and efficient than tailor-made solutions for each department	- Danger of frustrating specific work processes that do not 'fit in'
+ No 'grey areas' that allow negotiations about exceptions to the rule	

Some organizations function best in a conventional office, whereas others are better off in a flexible or even virtual office

Client Uniflair
Location Padua, Italy
Design Mario Cucinella Architects

WORK SPACES

In this chapter we provide an overview of various types of work space that can be found on typical office floors. It concerns spaces that are specifically designed or suitable for desk-related activities, such as reading, writing, telephoning and PC work. Per type of work space, we briefly touch on use and activities, size and layout, advantages and disadvantages as well as various considerations to keep in mind.

The most important distinction between the various work space types is their size and the degree to which they are enclosed; they range from small open offices to large enclosed offices. Therefore, the various types provide different degrees of visual privacy (the extent to which users can see others or can be seen by others) and acoustic privacy (the extent to which users can hear others or can be heard by others). These characteristics have a direct impact on the interaction between office workers and their ability to concentrate.

Another important distinction is related to the way workstations are used; are they allocated to one individual or shared by multiple employees? Several of the discussed work space types are generally used on an allocated basis, such as the cubicle or private office. Others are specifically intended for shared use, such as the study booth or work lounge.

To determine the recommended minimum floor area per type of work space we have used the following table as guidance:

Using this table, a basic workstation with a desk for PC work, paperwork and a filing cabinet will have a recommended minimum footprint of six square metres (65 sq. ft.). Similarly, a private office with two extra chairs for small meetings results in a minimum footprint of nine square metres (97 sq. ft.).

It is important to note that in the actual design, it might be recommendable to add additional square metres to floor area per workstation to increase flexibility. For example, making a shared office the same size as a private office enhances the interchangeability of these spaces.

Furthermore, it is important to acknowledge that the mentioned minimum sizes are very generic. In practice, the size of workstations is strongly influenced by local culture, regulations and costs. For example, work spaces in London or Hong Kong tend to be significantly smaller than those in Amsterdam or Stockholm, due to differences in business culture, regulations and the costs of space.

Recommended minimum space per workstation		
Basic space for writing and typing (e.g. desktop or laptop)	4 sq. m.	43 sq. ft.
Additional space to put paper on one side (e.g. in-tray space)	1 sq. m.	11 sq. ft.
Space for filing (for each filing cabinet)	1 sq. m.	11 sq. ft.
Space for meetings (for each additional chair)	1.5 sq. m.	16 sq. ft.

Client
BMW Group
Location
Munich, Germany
Design
Henn Architekten

High ceilings and double height glazing enhance access to daylight

Client
Burnkit
Location
Vancouver, Canada
Design
Burnkit

Raw and informal aesthetics match this company's youthful culture

Client
Wegener
Location
Apeldoorn, the Netherlands
Design
Ahrend

Acoustic ceilings and carpets help to reduce background noise

Open office

An open work space for more than ten
people, suitable for activities which
demand frequent communication or
routine activities which need relatively
little concentration

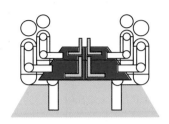

Use and activities
- Solo work requiring relatively little
  concentration, such as basic administration
- Collaborative work requiring frequent
  impromptu interaction between people
- Creative work requiring an atelier-like setting,
  such as architectural design

Size and layout
- The recommended minimum floor area is six
  square metres (65 sq. ft.) per workstation
- Avoid desk arrangements in which people sit
  with their back towards circulation routes

Location
- Preferably located close to the facade,
  providing outside view and daylight access
- Avoid adjacency to busy circulation routes or
  support spaces, such as print and copy areas,
  to prevent unnecessary distraction

Considerations
- Pay extra attention to acoustics (i.e. sound-
  absorbing materials, acoustic ceilings, sound
  masking)
- Depending on the type of work, it is
  recommended to combine open offices with
  additional shared study booths and meeting
  spaces
- A protocol for distracting activities, such as
  speaking on the telephone, listening to music
  and informal interaction, is recommended
- A protocol for tidiness and cleanliness might be
  considered since everything, from files to coffee
  cups, is directly visible in open offices

Alternative names
- Open-plan
- Office landscape

Advantages
+ Efficient utilization of space
+ Ability to increase density by adding extra desks
+ High degree of spatial flexibility (i.e. easy to
  reconfigure desk arrangements)
+ No physical barriers to communication,
  which can improve interaction and workplace
  learning

Disadvantages
- Limited acoustic and visual privacy
- Not suitable for work requiring confidentiality
- No possibilities for individual climate control

Client
BDP
Location
Manchester, United
Kingdom
Design
BDP

Filing cabinets are used to
create team spaces for up
to eight people

Client
INHolland University
Location
Rotterdam,
the Netherlands
Design
Hollandse Nieuwe

Bay configuration allows
users to interact by simply
turning their chairs

Client
Ahrend
Location
Amsterdam,
the Netherlands
Design
Ahrend

Bright team space with
filing and storage cabinets
that act as a noise buffer

Team space

A semi-enclosed work space for two
to eight people; suitable for teamwork
which demands frequent internal
communication and a medium level
of concentration

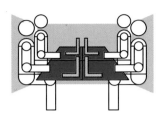

Use and activities
* Collaborative work requiring frequent
  interaction within teams
* Solo work requiring medium concentration,
  such as PC work

Size and layout
* The recommended minimum floor area is six
  square metres (65 sq. ft.) per workstation, or
  seven-and-a-half square metres (81 sq. ft.)
  when a meeting table is added
* Desks can be arranged face-to-face or back-
  to-back, respectively enhancing interaction or
  concentration

Location
* Preferably located close to the facade,
  providing outside view and daylight access
* Avoid adjacency to busy circulation routes or
  support spaces, such as break areas, to prevent
  unnecessary distraction

Considerations
* Carefully choose the height of partitions: low
  partitions add to openness, high partitions add
  to visual privacy
* Adding a small table in the middle of the space
  enables employees to start a meeting by simply
  turning their office chairs
* Pay extra attention to acoustics (i.e. sound-
  absorbing materials, acoustic ceiling or sound
  masking). Please note that partitions with a
  height of less than 1.5 metres (5 ft.) have little to
  no impact on acoustics
* A protocol for distracting activities, such as
  speaking on the telephone, listening to music
  and informal interaction, is recommended
* Depending on the type of work, it is
  recommended to combine team offices with
  additional shared study booths and meeting
  spaces

Alternative names
* Bullpen
* Cluster
* Pod

Advantages
+ Efficient utilization of space
+ Relatively flexible because medium-high
  partitions are easier to move than ceiling-high
  partitions
+ No physical barriers to communication within
  teams, which can improve interaction and
  workplace learning

Disadvantages
- Lack of acoustic privacy, limited visual privacy
- Not suitable for work requiring confidentiality
- No possibilities for individual climate control

Client
Alibaba
Location
Hangzhou, China
Design
Hassell

Cubicles allow for highly efficient use of the available space

Client
California Department of Transportation
Location
Los Angeles, United States
Design
Gruen Associates

Allocated cubicles allow for the personalization of individual workstations

Client
New York Times
Location
New York, United States
Design
Gensler

A large atrium brings daylight deep into the building and creates a sense of openness

Cubicle

A semi-enclosed work space for one person, suitable for activities which demand medium concentration and medium interaction

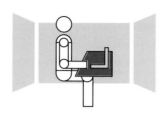

Use and activities
* Solo work requiring medium concentration, such as PC work
* Work requiring medium to little interaction between people

Size and layout
* The recommended minimum floor area is six square metres (65 sq. ft.) per workstation

Location
* Preferably located close to the facade, providing outside view and daylight access
* Avoid adjacency to busy circulation routes or support spaces, such as pantries, to prevent unnecessary distraction

Considerations
* Carefully choose the height of partitions: low partitions add to openness, high partitions add to visual privacy
* Pay extra attention to acoustics (i.e. sound-absorbing materials, acoustic ceiling or sound masking). Please note that partitions with a height of less than 1.5 metres (5 ft.) have little to no impact on acoustics
* A protocol for distracting activities, such as speaking on the telephone, listening to music and informal interaction, is recommended
* Cubicles have a relatively negative image among users

Alternative names
* Coupe
* Clipper

Advantages
+ Efficient utilization of space
+ Relatively flexible because medium-high partitions are easier to move than ceiling-high partitions

Disadvantages
- Limited acoustic and visual privacy
- Not very suitable for work requiring confidentiality
- Very few possibilities for individual climate control
- The highly individual character of cubicles can inhibit workplace learning and interaction

Client
Caballero Fabriek
Location
The Hague,
the Netherlands
Design
GROUP A

Transparent partitions
reduce the closed
character of private offices
and bring in daylight

Client
Design Council
Location
London, United Kingdom
Design
Clive Sall Architecture &
Carl Turner Architects

A management office with
a large window to preserve
a visual connection with
the rest of the office

Client
adidas & Reebok
Location
Amsterdam,
the Netherlands
Design
Hollandse Nieuwe

A private office that can
be used for meetings when
unoccupied

Private office

An enclosed work space for one person, suitable for activities which are confidential, demand a lot of concentration or include many small meetings

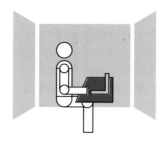

Use and activities
* Solo work requiring high concentration, such as analyzing complex information
* Work requiring a high degree of confidentiality, such as staff appraisals
* Work requiring many small meetings alternated with regular desk-based activities
* Activities that can be disturbing or distracting for others, such as telephone calls

Size and layout
* The recommended minimum floor area is nine square metres (97 sq. ft.) per workstation when providing space for both a desk and meetings with two people
* Preferably, the desk arrangement gives the user a direct sight of the door

Location
* Preferably located close to a window, providing outside view and daylight access
* Can be located near busy circulation routes or other open spaces when properly insulated

Considerations
* Mostly allocated for cultural reasons (status) or functional reasons (privacy)
* The utilization rate can be increased by fitting the office out as a meeting space
* Using transparent partitions reduces the closed character of private offices and brings more daylight into the building, but does, however, increase visual distraction

Alternative names
* Cellular office
* Management office

Advantages
+ Provides acoustic and visual privacy
+ Very suitable for work requiring confidentiality
+ Can be used as a marker of status
+ Can be used as a meeting room by others when empty
+ Excellent possibilities for individual climate control

Disadvantages
- Relatively expensive because enclosed offices demand more space and require enclosing walls
- Inflexible since ceiling-high partitions cannot easily be moved
- Danger of low utilization rate
- May block communication and knowledge exchange with co-workers, unless there is an 'open door culture'

Client
Dupon Real Estate
Development
Location
Hoofddorp,
the Netherlands
Design
Studio Ramin Visch

Light colours and large
windows create a feeling
of spaciousness

Client
Google
Location
Zurich, Switzerland
Design
Camenzind Evolution

Oak-effect door with
small porthole provides
additional visual privacy

Client
Degussa Creavis
Location
Marl, Germany
Design
Henn Architekten

Sharing should be by
people with a similar
working pattern and
attitude to work

Shared office

An enclosed work space for two
or three people, suitable for semi-
concentrated work and collaborative
work in small groups

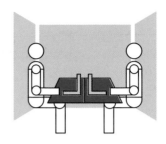

Use and activities
* Work requiring a mix of concentration and
  collaboration, such as collaborative research
  and development
* Collaborative work requiring frequent
  impromptu interaction between two or three
  people

Size and layout
* The recommended minimum floor area is six
  square metres (65 sq. ft.) per workstation, or
  seven-and-a-half square metres (81 sq. ft.)
  when a meeting table is added
* Desks can be arranged face-to-face or back-
  to-back, respectively enhancing interaction or
  concentration
* Preferably, the desk arrangement gives the
  inhabitants a direct sight of the door

Location
* Preferably located close to a window, providing
  outside view and daylight access
* Can be located near busy circulation routes or
  other open spaces when properly insulated

Considerations
* Mostly allocated for functional reasons
  (collaboration)
* Best shared by people having a similar working
  pattern and attitude to work

Alternative names
* Department room
* Group room
* Twin room

Advantages
+ Provides a reasonable amount of privacy and
  confidentiality among the room's users
+ Fairly good possibilities for individual climate
  control
+ Generally appreciated by users for balancing
  privacy and interaction

Disadvantages
- Relatively expensive because enclosed offices
  demand more space and require enclosing
  walls
- Inflexible since ceiling-high partitions cannot
  easily be moved
- Danger of low utilization rate when used as
  allocated workplaces
- May block communication and knowledge
  exchange with others than one's 'roommates',
  unless there is an 'open door culture'

Client
Cubion A/S
Location
Copenhagen, Denmark
Design
Jackie-B

Simple design interventions, using colours and prints, create a surprising work space

Client
Trust Creative Society
Location
Tampere, Finland
Design
Trust Creative Society

Furniture on wheels allows for easy reconfiguration of the room layout

Client
Microsoft
Location
Amsterdam, the Netherlands
Design
Sevil Peach

Collaborative work requires frequent impromptu interaction within teams

Team room

An enclosed work space for four to ten people; suitable for teamwork which may be confidential and demands frequent internal communication

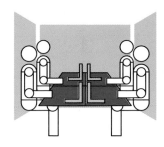

Use and activities
- Collaborative work requiring frequent interaction within teams
- Solo work requiring medium concentration, such as PC work
- Work requiring a certain degree of confidentiality, such as auditing

Size and layout
- The recommended minimum floor area is six square metres (65 sq. ft.) per workstation, or seven-and-a-half square metres (81 sq. ft.) when a meeting table is added
- Desks can be arranged face-to-face or back-to-back, respectively enhancing interaction or concentration
- Preferably, the desk arrangement gives the inhabitants a direct sight of the door

Location
- Preferably located close to a window, providing outside view and daylight access
- Can be located near busy circulation routes or other open spaces when properly insulated

Considerations
- Balancing the required levels of concentration and interaction can be problematic
- Typically equipped with white boards to facilitate interaction among the room's users
- Best shared with people having a similar working pattern and attitude to work

Alternative names
- Group office
- Project room
- Department room

Advantages
+ Provides a certain amount of privacy and confidentiality as well as team interaction
+ Team setting stimulates free flow of knowledge and workplace learning within teams
+ Fairly good possibilities for individual climate control

Disadvantages
- Floor-to-ceiling partitions negatively impact the cost efficiency and flexibility
- Danger of unpredictable utilization rates (i.e. intensively used during a particular project and empty when a project is finished)
- Teams are separated from the rest of the office

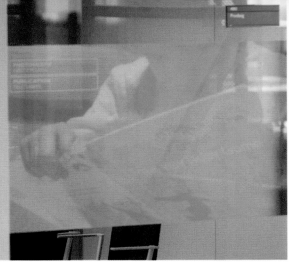

Client
BBC Scotland
Location
Glasgow, United Kingdom
Design
Graven Images

Separate spaces for phone calls reduce noise on the floor of open offices

Client
TNT
Location
The Hague, the Netherlands
Design
Fokkema & Partners Architecten

Unallocated study booth for short-term use (one to two hours)

Client
The Writable Office
Location
Seattle, United States
Design
Chadbourne + Doss Architects

Boxes for work requiring high concentration, located in the inner areas of the building

Study booth

An enclosed work space for one person; suitable for short-term activities which demand concentration or confidentiality

Use and activities
- Solo work requiring high concentration, such as assessing complex reports
- Work requiring a high degree of privacy, such as confidential conference calls
- Activities that can be disturbing or distracting for others such as telephone calls
- Mostly used on a bookable basis for temporary use by flexible or mobile employees

Size and layout
- The recommended minimum floor area is six square metres (65 sq. ft.) per workstation
- Preferably, the desk arrangement gives the user a direct sight of the door

Location
- Can be located in the inner areas of the building because it is intended for short-term use only

Considerations
- Careful planning is necessary to coordinate the demand of study booths (utilization rates vary strongly per organization)
- When too narrow, people might leave doors open, which negatively impacts the functionality
- Can be used for small meetings when equipped with an extra chair
- Avoid transparency from all sides to prevent a 'fish-bowl' effect

Alternative names
- Cockpit
- Quiet room
- Think tank

Advantages
+ Efficient utilization of space when frequently occupied
+ Provides a lot of privacy and confidentiality
+ Excellent possibilities for individual climate control

Disadvantages
- Difficult to guarantee availability when not used on a non-bookable basis
- Protocols for use are recommended, e.g. a booking system to avoid queuing

Client
Sabic Europe
Location
Sittard, the Netherlands
Design
GROUP A

Comfortable workstations,
providing some privacy
and room for informal
meetings

Client
BBC Worldwide
Location
London, United Kingdom
Design
DEGW

Used on a 'first come,
first served' basis for
temporary use by flexible
employees

Client
Spaces
Location
Amsterdam,
the Netherlands
Design
Sevil Peach

A work lounge enclosed by
medium-high partitions
with a sound-absorbing
finish

Work lounge

A lounge-like work space for two to six people; suitable for short-term activities which demand collaboration and/or allow impromptu interaction

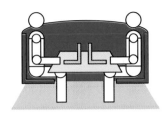

Use and activities
- Solo work requiring relatively little concentration, such as reading trade journals
- Collaborative work requiring informal interaction between a few people
- Mostly used on a 'first come, first served' basis for temporary use by flexible employees

Size and layout
- The recommended minimum floor area is four square metres (43 sq. ft.) per workstation

Location
- Can be located in the inner areas of the building because it is intended for short-term use only
- To support the informal use of these workplaces they can be located near circulation routes or support spaces, although this increases chances of distraction

Considerations
- Attractive design is likely to increase the utilization rate
- When designed as a single continuous bench people might hesitate joining another occupant

Alternative names
- Business centre
- Club

Advantages
+ Efficient utilization of space when frequently occupied
+ Can act as overflow space for peak periods of high occupancy
+ Enables discussions to take place away from open and semi-enclosed workstations
+ Can act as an attractive alternative in addition to allocated workstations

Disadvantages
- Limited privacy and confidentiality (i.e. noise and interruptions from adjacent spaces)
- No possibilities for individual climate control
- Fully adjustable lounge furniture can be rather expensive

Client
Student Loans Company
Location
Darlington, United
Kingdom
Design
3FOLD

When frequently occupied
this touch down area
provides a highly efficient
use of space

Client
Microsoft
Location
Amsterdam,
the Netherlands
Design
Sevil Peach

Cubicles with medium-
high partitions allow more
visual privacy when
checking e-mails

Client
VU University
Location
Amstelveen,
the Netherlands
Design
Hollandse Nieuwe

Standing-only touch
downs provide space for
quick tasks, such as
checking e-mails

Touch down

An open work space for one person; suitable for short-term activities which require little concentration and low interaction

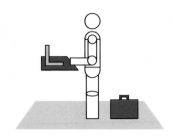

Use and activities
- Work requiring little time and little concentration, such as checking e-mails
- Mostly used on a 'first come, first served' basis for temporary use by mobile employees

Size and layout
- The recommended minimum floor area is four square metres (43 sq. ft.) per workstation

Location
- Can be located in the inner areas of the building because it is intended for short-term use only
- Preferably located near busy circulation routes, meeting spaces and support spaces

Considerations
- Attractive design is likely to increase the utilization rate
- Often designed to be used while standing, instead of sitting, underlining the short-term character of its use

Alternative names
- Internet spot
- Check point

Advantages
+ Efficient utilization of space when frequently occupied
+ Can act as overflow space for peak periods of high occupancy
+ High degree of spatial flexibility (i.e. relatively easy to add to existing layout)

Disadvantages
- Only suitable for a limited range of office activities
- Lack of acoustic and visual privacy
- No possibilities for individual climate control

In this increasingly virtual world, the office becomes a meeting space, rather than just a place to get work done

Client Loch Lomond
Location Balloch, United Kingdom
Design Loch Lomond & The Trossachs National Park Authority

MEETING SPACES

In this chapter we provide an overview of various types of meeting space that can be found on typical office floors. It concerns spaces that are specifically designed or suitable for various types of meeting for groups with a size ranging from two to twelve persons. With each type of meeting space, we briefly touch on use and activities, size and layout, advantages and disadvantages as well as various considerations to keep in mind.

The most important distinction between the various meeting space types is the number of users and the degree to which the space is open or enclosed. Another important discriminator is the character of the meeting space, which is related to the nature of the meeting. Different types of meeting (formal or informal, scheduled or impromptu) ask for different kinds of space.

To determine the recommended minimum floor area per type of meeting space we have used the following table as guidance:

Recommended minimum space per meeting space

Open meeting space	1.5 sq. m. / person	16 sq. ft. / person
Enclosed meeting space	2 sq. m. / person	22 sq. ft. / person
Meeting space with special equipment/furniture	3 sq. m. / person	32 sq. ft. / person
Meeting point where people stand	1 sq. m. / person	11 sq. ft. / person

Client
Formuepleje
Location
Aarhus, Denmark
Design
schmidt hammer lassen
architects

Transparent walls provide
overview, but may also
cause visual distraction

Client
Cubion A/S
Location
Copenhagen, Denmark
Design
Jackie-B

A round table and white
boards enable creative
sessions

Client
adidas & Reebok
Location
Amsterdam,
the Netherlands
Design
Hollandse Nieuwe

They help take distracting
meetings away from open
work spaces

Small meeting room

An enclosed meeting space for two to four persons, suitable for both formal and informal interaction

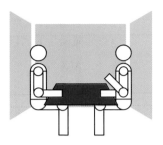

Use and activities
+ Suitable for small meetings
+ Suitable for confidential discussions
+ Often used on a 'first come, first served' basis

Size and layout
+ The recommended minimum floor area is two square metres (22 sq. ft.) per person
+ Can be equipped with technology enabling conference calls and/or video conferencing

Location
+ Can be located in the inner areas of the building because it is intended for short-term use only
+ Preferably located near work areas to take distracting interaction away from open work spaces
+ Avoid transparency from multiple sides to prevent a 'fish-bowl' effect

Considerations
+ The use of transparent walls can cause visual distraction when located near busy circulation routes
+ Provide these spaces in different sizes, locations and atmospheres
+ In open work settings, the provision of small meeting rooms contributes to a less disruptive work environment

Alternative names
+ Interview room
+ Drop-in room

Advantages
+ Size suits majority of scheduled meetings and confidential discussions
+ Can be used as bookable workstation (e.g. study booth) when not used for meetings

Disadvantages
- When used on a 'first come, first served' basis, availability cannot be guaranteed
- Due to its small size, not very suitable for presentations that require a data projector

Client
Nykredit
Location
Copenhagen, Denmark
Design
schmidt hammer lassen
architects

This meeting room 'floats'
into the building's main
atrium, creating a
stunning visual effect

Client
Trust Creative Society
Location
Tampere, Finland
Design
Trust Creative Society

This meeting room can
also be used as a work
space for project teams

Client
JWT
Location
New York, United States
Design
Clive Wilkinson Architects

Located at the facade, this
meeting room has access
to daylight and an outside
view

Large meeting room

An enclosed meeting space for five to twelve people, suitable for formal interaction

Use and activities
- Suitable for scheduled meetings with groups
- Suitable for confidential meetings
- Suitable for presentations
- In most cases centrally booked and maintained

Size and layout
- The recommended minimum floor area is two square metres (22 sq. ft.) per person
- The room layout should be such that all attendees face each other
- At least one wall should be suitable for projections
- Can be equipped with technology enabling presentations, conference calls and/or video conferencing

Location
- Preferably located at the facade, providing outside view and daylight access
- Preferably located near a floor entrance (i.e. lift or staircase) to create short walking distances and avoid unnecessary distraction for people working on the generic office floors

- Preferably located near a pantry area, making the provision of coffee and tea for large groups easier
- Preferably located near a break area or spacious corridor where pre- and after-meeting discussions can take place

Considerations
- The use of transparent walls can cause visual distraction when located near busy circulation routes
- Extra space and the use of flexible furniture enables users to make different meeting configurations (theatre, cabaret, horseshoe) for different types of meetings

Alternative names
- Conference room
- Seminar room
- Boardroom

Advantages
+ Can be converted to smaller rooms when folding walls are used
+ Can also be used as a brainstorming room when properly equipped
+ Can also be used as work space for project teams when space is scarce

Disadvantages
- Needs rules for use and policy for no-shows
- Utilization tends to be high at certain times only (i.e. between 10am and 11am and between 3pm and 4pm)

Client
Cubion A/S
Location
Copenhagen, Denmark
Design
Jackie-B

A meeting space with an open, yet clearly defined framework of walls and a roof

Client
BBC Scotland
Location
Glasgow, United Kingdom
Design
Graven Images

Fully open meeting space, located in the middle of the work floor to facilitate impromptu interaction

Client
JWT
Location
New York, United States
Design
Clive Wilkinson Architects

The curtain provides a certain degree of visual privacy and absorbs background noise

Small meeting space

An open or semi-open meeting space
for two to four persons; suitable for
short, informal interaction

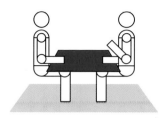

Use and activities
* Suitable for small ad hoc meetings
* Suitable for non-confidential discussions
* Often used on 'first come, first served' basis

Size and layout
* The recommended minimum floor area is one-and-a-half square metres (16 sq. ft.) per person

Location
* Can be located in the inner areas of the building because of its informal use
* Preferably located near work spaces to facilitate impromptu interaction
* Another option is to locate it near a support space, such as a pantry, to stimulate informal communication when chance encounters take place

Considerations
* Medium-high partitions or curtains create visual privacy
* Provide these spaces in different sizes, locations and atmospheres
* Utilization rate largely dependent on location and finishing
* Usage by employees from other floors or departments is often regarded as intrusive

Alternative names
* Break-out area
* Huddle

Advantages
+ Size suits majority of ad hoc meetings and non-confidential discussions
+ Encourages informal meetings and networking since there is no need to book in advance
+ Can be used as informal workstation (e.g. touch down) or waiting area when not used for meetings

Disadvantages
- Due to its informal use, availability cannot be guaranteed
- Noise can be distracting to adjacent staff
- Lack of privacy and confidentiality

Client
IT-University Copenhagen
Location
Ørestaden, Denmark
Design
Bosch & Fjord

A movable set of wooden
boxes allows for different
settings for informal
interaction

Client
Unilever Benelux
Location
Rotterdam,
the Netherlands
Design
newCreations

A non-confidential
presentation where
curtains provide visual
privacy

Client
ABITARE
Location
Milan, Italy
Design
Cibic and Partners

Meeting space located
next to the pantry area – a
natural spot for gatherings

Large meeting space

An open or semi-open meeting space for five to twelve people; suitable for short, informal interaction

Use and activities
* Suitable for large informal meetings
* Suitable for non-confidential meetings and presentations
* Suitable for workplace 'rituals', such as birthday parties
* Often used on 'first come, first served' basis

Size and layout
* The recommended minimum floor area is one-and-a-half square metres (16 sq. ft.) per person
* The layout should be such that all attendees face each other

Location
* Can be located in the inner areas of the building because of its informal use
* Preferably located near work spaces to facilitate impromptu interaction

Considerations
* Medium-high partitions or curtains create visual privacy
* A protocol for ownership of the space and its cleaning is recommended
* Utilization rate largely dependent on location and finishing
* Usage by employees from other floors or departments is often regarded as intrusive

Alternative names
* Project space
* Training area

Advantages
+ Encourages informal meetings and networking (i.e. people passing by can easily join meetings)
+ No need to book in advance
+ Can be used as informal workstation (e.g. touch down) or waiting area when not used for meetings

Disadvantages
- Due to its informal use, availability cannot be guaranteed
- Noise can be distracting to adjacent staff
- Lack of privacy and confidentiality

Client
Momentum
Location
Hørsholm, Denmark
Design
Bosch & Fjord

Ample wall space to
visualize ideas and flexible
furniture to reconfigure
the room layout

Client
Twynstra Gudde
Location
Amersfoort,
the Netherlands
Design
YNNO

A space that allows for
'messy' brainstorm
sessions and workshops

Client
Dutch Central
Government
Location
The Hague,
the Netherlands
Design
Hollandse Nieuwe

Brainstorming in a
'homey' environment with
kitchen table, flowers and
even candles

Brainstorm room

An enclosed meeting space for
five to twelve persons; suitable
for brainstorming sessions and
workshops

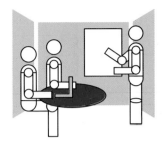

Use and activities
* Suitable for brainstorming sessions and workshops
* Suitable for semi-confidential presentations and discussions
* In most cases centrally booked and maintained

Size and layout
* The recommended minimum floor area is three square metres (32 sq. ft.) per person
* The room layout should be such that all attendees face each other
* At least one wall should be suitable for projections
* Typically well-equipped with flexible furniture, flip charts, white boards and/or smart boards enabling creativity and innovation

Location
* Preferably located at the facade, providing outside view and daylight access
* Preferably located near break areas and/or pantry areas

Considerations
* Extra space and the use of flexible furniture enables users to make different meeting configurations (theatre, cabaret, horseshoe) for different types of meetings
* Distinctive finishing and furniture provide the room with a unique atmosphere

Alternative names
* Innovation room
* Strategy room
* Creative space

Advantages
+ Can also be used as a large meeting room when properly equipped
+ Can stimulate creativity and innovation when properly designed and equipped

Disadvantages
- Danger of unpredictable utilization rates

Client
LEGO Group
Location
Billund, Denmark
Design
Bosch & Fjord

A high table to facilitate
brief interactions and
comfy cushions to relax
and unwind

Client
BBC Scotland
Location
Glasgow, United Kingdom
Design
Graven Images

A narrow table that takes
away the distance and
formality of conventional
meetings

Client
Ministry of Education,
Culture and Science
Location
The Hague,
the Netherlands
Design
OTH & YNNO

This meeting point
doubles as both a waiting
area for visitors and touch
down for employees

Meeting point

An open meeting point for two to four persons; suitable for ad hoc, informal meetings

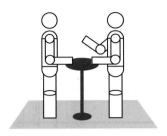

Use and activities
+ Suitable for small and short ad hoc meetings
+ Suitable for non-confidential discussions
+ Used on 'first come, first served' basis

Size and layout
+ The recommended minimum floor area is one square metre (11 sq. ft.) per person

Location
+ Can be located in the inner areas of the building because of its informal use
+ Located near or within break areas, pantry areas or circulation areas

Considerations
+ Design and quality of furniture positively impacts the utilization rate
+ Provide these spaces in different sizes, locations and atmospheres

Alternative names
+ Chat point
+ Bird table

Advantages
+ Facilitates chance encounters and impromptu meetings
+ Can be used as a waiting area for visitors
+ Meeting points take up very little space

Disadvantages
- Utilization largely dependent on location and finishing
- Noise can be distracting to adjacent staff
- Limited privacy and confidentiality

Support spaces tend to attract a random variety of people and can therefore act as a powerful tool to stimulate interaction

Client SJ Berwin
Location London, United Kingdom
Design HOK

SUPPORT SPACES

In this chapter we provide an overview of various types of support space that can be found on typical office floors. It concerns spaces that are specifically designed to support the various work processes that take place in an ordinary office building. Per type of support space, we briefly touch on use and activities, size and layout, advantages and disadvantages as well as various considerations to keep in mind.

The need for this type of space will depend on the work processes and organization. For example, an organization with highly digitalized work processes will need less filing space than an organization that still works with paper. Furthermore, organizational culture will play a large role. A 'games room', for example, may in one company be regarded as an essential element of the company culture and in another as completely irrelevant and a waste of space.

An important consideration when designing support spaces is their social potential. Many support spaces act as meeting points. Think of the casual meetings and chance encounters that take place at the water-cooler or copy machine. Thereby, such spaces can positively impact on internal communication and social cohesion within organizations.

To make optimal use of the 'magnet function' of support spaces, they should be strategically positioned. Creating too many support spaces decreases the intensity of use and, consequently, the chance of social interaction. Creating a limited number of 'service points', at busy traffic routes (e.g. near stairs and lifts) and the combination of different support functions (e.g. pantry, copier and mail) is more effective.

Please note: the sizes of the different support spaces that are mentioned in this chapter are indicative. The actual size of a support space, such as a break area, depends strongly on the number of people using it.

Client
TNT
Location
The Hague,
the Netherlands
Design
Fokkema & Partners
Architecten

If designed with acoustic
properties, filing cabinets
can act as a noise buffer

Client
Formuepleje
Location
Aarhus, Denmark
Design
schmidt hammer lassen
architects

Shared filing in the
corridor with cabinets low
enough not to block sight
lines

Client
Unilever Supply Chain
Company
Location
Schaffhausen, Switzerland
Design
newCreations

A design folly that prevents
a 'messy' atmosphere in
the work environment

Filing space

An open or enclosed support space for the storage of frequently used files and documents

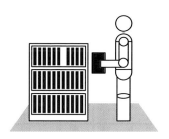

Use and activities
- Storage and management of frequently used documents and files such as reference documents and personnel files
- Can also be used as storage space when under-utilized

Size and layout
- The recommended minimum floor area is one square metre (11 sq. ft.) per filing cabinet (including clearance for proper access to the cabinet)
- In many projects the available shelf space is limited to one linear metre (3 ft.) per person – please note that the actual need strongly depends on the degree of digitalization and the type of work processes

Location
- The recommended maximum walking distance from any workstation is ten metres (33 ft.), but it is preferably located in the direct vicinity of work spaces
- Can be located in the inner areas of the building since there is no need for daylight access

Considerations
- The need for filing space is directly related to the discussion about the digitalization of work processes and flexible working
- With increasingly mature IT solutions, physical filing is likely to become obsolete at some point. But for now, do not underestimate people's fondness for personal files and paper documents; decreasing the amount of filing space only works when digital alternatives are available and user-friendly
- Large filing cabinets (e.g. carousel filing systems) add significantly to the internal weight load on office floors
- A protocol for periodic clean-ups of filing cabinets can support space efficiency
- Open filing cabinets may add to a 'messy' atmosphere in the office

Alternative names
- Local archive
- Live filing

Advantages
+ Can be used as space divider and act as noise buffer (when higher than one-and-a-half metres (5 ft.) and fitted with acoustic properties such as perforations in back panels and front doors)
+ Space efficient when clearance area overlaps with secondary circulation space

Disadvantages
- Filing spaces are rather 'unproductive' square metres of costly office space with no other function than the storage of files and documents
- The use of high cabinets can block sight lines and access to daylight

Client
Design Council
Location
London, United Kingdom
Design
Clive Sall Architecture &
Carl Turner Architects

Storage combined with
personal filing cabinet
and located adjacent to
workstation

Client
AK Bank
Location
Amsterdam,
the Netherlands
Design
dagli+ atelier
d'architecture

Storage space which is
elegantly integrated into
a room's dividing wall

Client
BBC Worldwide
Location
London, United Kingdom
Design
DEGW

The clearance area
overlaps with secondary
circulation space creating
an efficient use of space

Storage space

An open or enclosed support space for the storage of commonly used office supplies

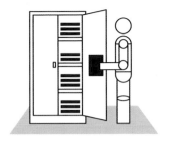

Use and activities
- Storage and provision of commonly used office supplies, such as folders and markers
- Can also be used for the storage of other material, such as corporate brochures and business cards

Size and layout
- The recommended minimum number of storage spaces is one per floor or department, depending on how the provision of office supplies is organized
- The recommended minimum floor area is one square metre (11 sq. ft.) per storage cabinet (including clearance for proper access to the cabinet)

Location
- The recommended maximum walking distance from any workstation is 50 metres (164 ft.)
- Can be located in the inner areas of the building since there is no need for daylight access
- Often combined with print and copy area and mail area to form a central 'service point'

- Located near department's secretariat when they are responsible for stocking office supplies

Considerations
- Make someone responsible for managing the stock of office supplies
- Consider whether storage areas, or the cabinets located in these areas, should be lockable or supervised to prevent misuse
- Large storage cabinets (e.g. movable shelving systems) add significantly to the internal weight load on office floors
- A protocol for periodic clean-ups of filing cabinets can support space efficiency
- Regularly combined with print and copy area and mail area to enhance chance encounters

Alternative names
- Stockroom
- Team storage

Advantages
+ Centralized storage space reduces the amount of office supplies in personal desk pedestals
+ Enclosed storage spaces keep office supplies and other material out of sight and contribute to a neat and orderly atmosphere
+ Space efficient when clearance area overlaps with secondary circulation space
+ Efficient utilization of space when combined with print and copy area and mail area to form a central 'service point'

Disadvantages
- Storage spaces are rather 'unproductive' square metres of costly office space with no other function than the storage of office supplies
- Danger of being used for the storage of just anything

Client
YNNO Creative Valley
Location
Utrecht, the Netherlands
Design
SPRIKK & YNNO

This print and copy area is
properly shielded from
work spaces to avoid
distraction and disruption

Client
Waterschap Rivierenland
Location
Tiel, the Netherlands
Design
AGS Architekten

A service point where
printing and copying is
combined with storage
and mail

Client
British Petroleum
Location
London, United Kingdom
Design
Swanke Hayden Connell
Architects

This print and copy area
provides sufficient
surfaces for sorting out
papers

Print and copy area

An open or enclosed support space
with facilities for printing, scanning
and copying

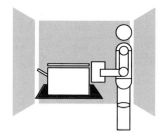

Use and activities
- Printing, copying, scanning and other
  paperwork such as sorting and binding
- Regularly combined with facilities for waste
  collection
- Chance encounters and casual conversations

Size and layout
- The recommended minimum number of print
  and copy areas is one per floor, or one per 50
  workstations, depending on the speed and
  capacity of the copier
- The recommended minimum floor area is six
  square metres (65 sq. ft.) per copier (including
  clearance for proper use of a medium-sized
  multifunctional). Please note that the actual
  area strongly depends on the possible placing
  of a side table to sort papers, facilities for waste
  collection and storage space for paper

Location
- The recommended maximum walking distance
  from any workstation is 50 metres (164 ft.)
- Can be located in the inner areas of the
  building since there is no need for daylight

- Preferably shielded from open and semi-
  enclosed work spaces to avoid distraction and
  disruption
- Often combined with storage space and mail
  area to form a central 'service point'
- Located near department's secretariat when
  they are responsible for stocking paper

Considerations
- With increasingly mature IT solutions such
  as e-books and digital ink, printers are likely
  to become obsolete at some point. For now,
  however, do not underestimate people's
  fondness for printing and copying documents
- A protocol for malfunctioning of printers
  and tidiness of the print and copy area is
  recommended
- Regularly combined with storage space and
  mail area to enhance chance encounters

Alternative names
- Service point
- Resource centre

Advantages
+ Centralized print and copy areas diminish the
  need for personal printers and discourage
  unnecessary paper usage
+ Can enhance unplanned and informal
  interaction
+ Space efficient when clearance area overlaps
  with secondary circulation space
+ Efficient utilization of space when combined
  with storage space and mail area to form a
  central 'service point'

Disadvantages
- Printers and copiers produce noise, add to
  internal heat load, and may emit toxic particles
- Possible issues with tidiness and confidential
  printing (the latter can be resolved by
  passwords)

Client
Stichting MEE
Location
Utrecht, the Netherlands
Design
Veldhoen + Company

Mailboxes combined with personal lockers create an efficient use of space

Client
Caballero Fabriek
Location
The Hague,
the Netherlands
Design
GROUP A

Cleverly located mail area at a central location that employees pass when entering the office

Client
Ministry of Economic Affairs
Location
The Hague,
the Netherlands
Design
Rijksgebouwendienst

Mail area is located near the secretary responsible for incoming and outgoing mail

Mail area

An open or semi-open support space
where employees can pick up or
deliver their personal mail

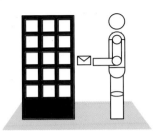

Use and activities
- Collection and delivery of incoming and
  outgoing mail

Size and layout
- The recommended minimum number of
  mail areas is one per floor or department,
  depending on how the collection and
  distribution of mail is organized
- The actual size of the mail area depends
  strongly on the number of 'pigeon-holes'
  and the type of cabinet

Location
- The recommended maximum walking distance
  from any workstation is 50 metres (164 ft.)
- Ideally situated at a central location that
  employees pass when entering the office
- Can be located in the inner areas of the
  building since there is no need for daylight
  access
- Often combined with storage space and print
  and copy area to form a central 'service point'
- Located near department's secretariat
  when they are responsible for incoming and
  outgoing mail

Considerations
- With increasingly mature IT solutions and
  central scanning facilities, physical mail is
  rapidly becoming obsolete, but people may
  still receive books, brochures and magazines
- Closed mailboxes are recommended when
  privacy or confidentiality is required
- Regularly combined with storage space
  and print and copy area to enhance chance
  encounters

Alternative names
- Mail drop
- Pigeon-hole

Advantages
- + Centralized mail areas contribute to more
  efficient mail logistics
- + Space efficient when clearance area overlaps
  with secondary circulation space
- + Efficient utilization of space when combined
  with storage space and print and copy area to
  form a central 'service point'

Disadvantages
- - Mailboxes are rather 'unproductive' square
  metres of costly office space with no other
  function than the temporary storage of mail

Client
Coloplast
Location
Humlebæk, Denmark
Design
Bosch & Fjord

A pantry combined with the break area to stimulate unplanned and informal interaction

Client
BDP
Location
Manchester, United Kingdom
Design
BDP

A kitchenette with space for informal interaction, located directly next to open work spaces

Client
Waterschap Rivierenland
Location
Tiel, the Netherlands
Design
AGS Architekten

A cleverly located pantry that enhances chance encounters and casual conversations

Pantry area

An open or enclosed support space where people can get coffee and tea as well as soft drinks and snacks

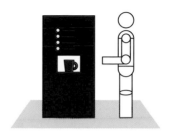

Use and activities
* Obtaining beverages and packaged food
* Regularly combined with a facility for recycling cups and cans and a kitchenette
* Chance encounters and casual conversations

Size and layout
* The recommended minimum number of pantry areas is one per floor, or one per 50 workstations, depending on the capacity of the vending machine
* The recommended minimum floor area is one-and-a-half square metres (16 sq. ft.) per vending machine plus one square metre (11 sq. ft.) per person using the machine or waiting in line

Location
* The recommended maximum walking distance from any workstation is 50 metres (164 ft.)
* Can be located in the inner areas of the building since there is no need for daylight access
* Preferably located in or near a break area and busy circulation routes

* Can be located near meeting spaces to enhance unplanned and informal interaction
* Preferably shielded from open and semi-open work spaces to avoid distraction and disruption

Considerations
* Level of luxury can vary from standard coffee machine to complete espresso bar and can be varied throughout the office to provide different levels of attractiveness
* Pay attention to the quality of the beverages and packaged food provided as the quality of products provided in the pantry area tends to be a much discussed topic in organizations
* The products provided in the pantry area can be seen in relation to a company's health policy (e.g. by providing fruit juices and healthy snacks)
* A protocol for tidiness and cleanliness is recommended

Alternative names
* Coffee corner
* Vending area

Advantages
+ Takes personal coffee-makers away from the work floor
+ Encourages informal interaction and networking
+ Space efficient when combined with break area

Disadvantages
- Can cause distraction and disruption to adjacent staff when designed as an open space
- Issues with tidiness (can be resolved by protocols and additional cleaning)

Client
LEGO Group
Location
Billund, Denmark
Design
Bosch & Fjord

Café-like break area that can also be used for casual meetings or as temporary workstations

Client
Kromann Reumert
Location
Copenhagen, Denmark
Design
schmidt hammer lassen architects

A spacious break area that can also be used for large company gatherings

Client
VU University
Location
Amstelveen,
the Netherlands
Design
Hollandse Nieuwe

A break area that doubles as both a waiting area and information centre

Break area

A semi-open or enclosed support space where employees can take a break from their work

Use and activities
* Taking a break from work
* Workplace 'rituals', such as office parties
* Can also be used for meetings or temporary use by mobile employees

Size and layout
* The recommended minimum number of break areas is one per 100 workstations, depending on the culture of the organization
* The recommended minimum floor area for break areas is two square metres (22 sq. ft.) per seat

Location
* The recommended maximum walking distance from any workstation is 50 metres (164 ft.)
* Can be located in the inner areas of the building since there is no need for daylight access
* Preferably located in or near a break area and busy circulation routes
* Can be located near meeting spaces to enhance unplanned and informal interaction
* Preferably shielded from open and semi-open work spaces to avoid distraction and disruption

Considerations
* Fit-out can vary from basic quality to high quality with comfortable seats and designer furniture
* Can also be used as reading room for employees or waiting area for visitors
* A protocol for tidiness and cleanliness is recommended

Alternative names
* Break out
* Relaxation area

Advantages
+ Provides a place for people to relax and unwind, away from their workstations
+ Can facilitate informal meetings and networking
+ Space efficient when combined with pantry area
+ Efficient utilization of space when designed as a multifunctional space (with informal work areas)

Disadvantages
- Can cause distraction and disruption to adjacent staff when designed as an open space
- Issues with tidiness (can be resolved by protocols and additional cleaning)
- Danger of low utilization when taking breaks is seen as 'not done'

Client
Microsoft
Location
Amsterdam,
the Netherlands
Design
Sevil Peach

Lockers with hand-written
names combined with
mailboxes to create an
efficient use of space

Client
BT Global Services
Location
Amsterdam,
the Netherlands
Design
GROUP A

Personal lockers cleverly
combined with coat-
hanging space

Client
Tax and Customs
Administration
Location
Arnhem, the Netherlands
Design
Sander Architecten

Cleverly situated lockers
at a central location that
employees pass when
entering the office

Locker area

An open or semi-open support space where employees can store their personal belongings

Use and activities
* Storage of personal belongings such as 'flexi-cases', laptops and mobile phones as well as personal documents, coats and umbrellas

Size and layout
* The recommended minimum number of locker areas is one per floor or department
* The actual size of the locker space depends on the number of lockers and the type of cabinet

Location
* The recommended maximum walking distance from any workstation is 50 metres (164 ft.)
* Ideally situated in a central location that employees pass when entering the office
* Can be located in the inner areas of the building since there is no need for daylight access

Considerations
* Especially with non-allocated work spaces, it is important to consider what type of locker space should be provided – locker spaces can vary from rather space-consuming 'garages', where employees store their trolleys, to small 'pigeon-holes', where they can store a single briefcase

Alternative names
* Personal garage
* Cloakroom

Advantages
+ Facilitates flexible and mobile working and enables staff to travel light
+ Reduces the need for personal desk pedestals
+ Space efficient when clearance area overlaps with secondary circulation space

Disadvantages
- Danger of low utilization when people have few personal belongings and bring their own briefcase to work

Client
Nykredit
Location
Copenhagen, Denmark
Design
schmidt hammer lassen
architects

A specially-designed
'smoking table' in the
main atrium

Client
Ministry of Agriculture,
Nature and Food Quality
Location
Assen, the Netherlands
Design
Bulder & Van der Most

A smoking room
combined with break area
and intelligent use of
coloured walls

Client
Interpolis
Location
Tilburg, the Netherlands
Design
Veldhoen + Company

This room takes smokers
away from the building's
entrance

Smoking room

An enclosed support space where employees can smoke a cigarette

Use and activities
- Smoking cigarettes and cigars
- Chance encounters and casual conversations

Size and layout
- If an organization chooses to have a smoking room, the recommended minimum number of smoking rooms is one per floor, or one per 100 workstations, depending on the company's smoking policy
- The recommended minimum floor area for smoking rooms is 1.2 square metres (13 sq. ft.) per smoker

Location
- The recommended maximum walking distance from any workstation is 100 metres (328 ft.)
- Preferably located at the facade, providing an outside view and daylight access
- Ideally located near a break area and/or a pantry, but not adjacent to busy circulation routes

Considerations
- Smoking rooms are increasingly banned from office buildings (in some countries they are prohibited)
- Coloured walls and hard-surface floors are preferred as white walls colour quickly and carpets collect smoke
- An alternative to a smoking room is a designated balcony or rooftop area, away from the entrance of a building

Alternative names
- Smokers lounge
- Smoking cabin

Advantages
+ Takes smokers (and their cigarette stubs) away from the entrance of the building

Disadvantages
- Requires additional technical installations for room ventilation
- Issues with tidiness and the smell of cigarette smoke
- Does not encourage smokers to kick their habit

Client
LEGO Group
Location
Billund, Denmark
Design
Bosch & Fjord

A library that can also be used for meetings or temporary use by mobile employees

Client
JWT
Location
New York, United States
Design
Clive Wilkinson Architects

Task lighting and colourful sofas give this library a comfortable 'touch and feel' vibe

Client
Kromann Reumert
Location
Copenhagen, Denmark
Design
schmidt hammer lassen architects

Circular bookcases create secluded spaces on an otherwise open floor

Library

A semi-open or enclosed support space for reading of books, journals and magazines

Use and activities
- Work that requires concentration, such as reading, writing and studying
- Can also be used for informal meetings when properly equipped
- Regularly combined with work lounges and touch downs

Size and layout
- The recommended minimum floor area of a library space is one square metre (11 sq. ft.) per book cabinet plus three square metres (32 sq. ft.) per study place

Location
- The recommended maximum walking distance from any workstation is 100 metres (328 ft.)
- Preferably located at the facade, providing an outside view and daylight access

Considerations
- Libraries are becoming increasingly obsolete with on-line availability of books and journals
- A protocol for ownership of the space and its tidiness is recommended
- Protocols for use are recommended, e.g. bringing library materials to work spaces
- A protocol for distracting activities such as telephoning and informal interaction is desirable

Alternative names
- Reading room
- Study area

Advantages
+ Provides a quiet place for activities requiring concentration, away from open workstations
+ Efficient utilization of space when designed to be multifunctional (with informal work spaces)

Disadvantages
- Danger of low utilization rates, depending on the culture and work style of the organization

Client
PayPal
Location
San Jose,
United States
Design
studio o+a

Space to relax and unwind:
low chairs, soft lighting
and board games

Client
Google
Location
Zurich, Switzerland
Design
Camenzind Evolution

Computer games may
require special attention
to soundproofing

Client
Headvertising
Location
Bucharest, Romania
Design
Corvin Christian

Some games, like table
tennis, require an ample
provision of space

Games room

An enclosed support space where
employees can play games (e.g.
computer games, pool, darts)

Use and activities
* Playing games
* Taking a break from work
* Social interaction with colleagues

Size and layout
* Sizes vary and depend on the games facilitated
  and the number of people participating (i.e.
  large rooms for pool or table tennis, smaller
  rooms for computer games)

Location
* Can be located in the inner areas of the
  building since there is no need for daylight
  access
* Ideally located in or near a pantry area
* Preferably shielded from open or semi-
  enclosed work spaces to avoid distraction and
  disruption

Considerations
* May ask for special attention to soundproofing
* Fit-out can vary from one specific game to a
  range of table games and video games
* A protocol for tidiness and cleanliness is
  recommended

Alternative names
* Fun room
* Entertainment room

Advantages
+ Provides a chance to relax and play, to take a
  sociable break during pressurized work days,
  helping to reduce stress-related complaints
+ Can positively affect staff morale and social
  cohesion
+ Can attract younger employees
+ Can be used as an expression of an informal
  and 'fun' organizational culture
+ Facilitates networking and informal meetings

Disadvantages
- Games rooms might be considered as
  'unproductive' square metres of costly office
  space
- Danger of low utilization, depending on the
  culture and work style of the organization

Client
Svenska Dagbladet
Location
Stockholm, Sweden
Design
Sweco FFNS

This waiting area is located at a central point that employees pass when entering the office

Client
BBC Scotland
Location
Glasgow, United Kingdom
Design
Graven Images

Giant cushions create an unconventional waiting area where visitors can 'chill'

Client
Ropewalks
Location
Macclesfield, United Kingdom
Design
BDP

Partitions with slogans and images provide visitors with a first impression of the organization

Waiting area

An open or semi-open support space where visitors can be received and can wait for their appointment

Use and activities
* Waiting
* Reading magazines/brochures
* Using laptop, blackberry or telephone
* Watching news or other media

Size and layout
* The recommended minimum number of waiting areas is one per floor or building
* The recommended minimum floor area is two square metres (22 sq. ft.) per seat

Location
* Near the entrance to the building or floor (staircase/elevators)
* Close to a reception desk or secretariat
* In the vicinity of sanitary facilities

Considerations
* Fit-out can vary from basic quality to high quality with comfortable seats and designer furniture
* Provision of multimedia, wireless Internet access and/or magazines can make a waiting area more attractive and functional
* A protocol for ownership of the space and keeping displayed materials and newspapers up-to-date is recommended

Alternative names
* Guest area
* 'Meet and greet'

Advantages
+ Provides a dedicated place for visitors to wait, keeping them from lingering on the office floor
+ Can help visitors to feel welcome
+ Can be used for branding, giving visitors a first impression of the organization

Disadvantages
- Waiting areas are rather 'unproductive' square metres of costly office space

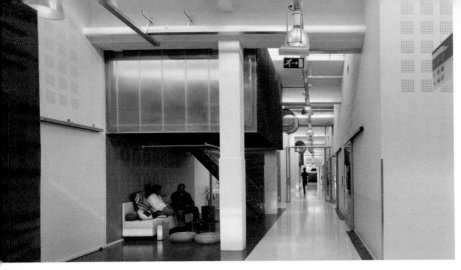

Client
Caballero Fabriek
Location
The Hague,
the Netherlands
Design
GROUP A

Lounges and spacious
corridors provide venues
for people to get together

Client
Ministry of Agriculture,
Nature and Food Quality
Location
The Hague,
the Netherlands
Design
BroekBakema &
Rijksgebouwendienst

Semi-open partitions
create a lively street with
traffic, views and chance
encounters

Client
Degussa Creavis
Location
Marl, Germany
Design
Henn Architekten

Open staircases
enhance
interdepartmental
interaction

Circulation space

Support space which is required for circulation on office floors, linking all major functions

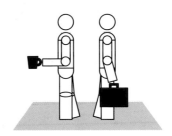

Use and activities
* Moving through the building
* Pacing up and down or wandering around
* Chance encounters and informal interaction

Size and layout
* The recommended amount of (primary) circulation space is between 10 and 15 per cent of the overall usable floor area
* For corridors a minimum width of 1.2 metres (4 ft.) is recommended

Location
* Can be located in the inner areas of the building since there is no need for daylight access
* Busy traffic routes should preferably be located away from open and semi-open work spaces to avoid distraction and disruption

Considerations
* Avoid dark, long and empty corridors. Try to create a 'street': lively spaces with traffic, views and encounters
* Clear signage helps people (especially visitors) to find their way
* Carefully selected materials and/or colours in flooring can aid navigation
* Sight lines (also to the outside) can aid orientation
* Short distances and obstacle-free circulation space are crucial for a building's fire safety. Compliance with local fire regulations is key (especially relevant when adding extra functions)
* Also pay attention to vertical circulation space: open staircases and atria can help communication across different floors

Alternative names
* Primary circulation
* Corridor

Advantages
+ Connects functions and spaces that are otherwise isolated
+ Can also be used as print/copy area, waiting area or informal meeting space, when sufficiently wide
+ Can be used as exhibition space for art, brand expressions or promotional material
+ Can enhance unplanned and informal interaction when carefully designed

Disadvantages
- Badly designed circulation spaces are rather 'unproductive' square metres of costly office space
- Busy traffic routes, and corridors where people tend to gather, can cause distraction and disruption to adjacent staff

One of the most critical steps in developing a new office concept is the positioning of all spaces and functions on the floor plate

Client Vidyalankar Institute of Technology
Location Mumbai, India
Design Planet 3 Studios

EXAMPLES

Once the objectives have been set, all crucial choices have been made and the key office spaces required have been selected, one can start to develop a zoning plan and ultimately a final design solution. Taking such a step-by-step approach, this chapter illustrates how the contents of this book can be brought together in practice.

Although this process can result in numerous design solutions, we would like to highlight four commonly found examples.

* Example A: an efficient landscape office for a large insurance company
* Example B: an attractive cellular office for a research and development centre
* Example C: a creative combination office for a successful media company
* Example D: a vibrant club office for a network of young companies

In line with the structured format of this book, each example will be explained using the following steps (which may also help to phase the project).

1 Objectives: what does the organization want to achieve with the new office environment?
2 Crucial choices: which strategic choices have been made in respect to the office concept?
3 Office spaces: what office space types best support the objectives set and choices made?
4 Zoning plan: how can these office spaces best be arranged on the available floor space?
5 Design solution: how can all previous steps be brought together in a concrete office design?

Although based on extensive experience in programming office buildings, please note that this chapter provides theoretical examples only. Developing fruitful design solutions is more complex in reality. However, we aim to illustrate how the previous chapters can be brought together in realistic solutions for office buildings.

Efficient landscape office

Business process re-engineering at a circa 1,000 staff back-office of this large insurance firm led to the refurbishment of their 1980s building, comprising 9,120 square metres (98,170 sq. ft.) spread over four storeys. The organizational overhaul and rebranding of the company led to the creation of a large open, flexible and highly efficient work environment.

To stand out in the increasingly competitive insurance industry, the entire process of concluding insurance policies all the way through handling and paying claims was revised to realize significant efficiency gains. It was decided to fully digitalize the entire process, create a new brand image and give employees much more individual responsibility in their work, doing away with unnecessary layers of hierarchy and departmental barriers.

Contextual facts
- Large insurance company
- Back-office with 1,000 staff
- BPR and full refurbishment
- 1980s four-storey building

OBJECTIVES – The existing interior of the building was a hotch potch of smaller and larger group rooms, filled with large filing cabinets, not up to the task of supporting the new way of working. In line with the organizational changes that were taking place, three objectives were selected for their new accommodation strategy: cost reduction, enhanced interaction and expression of the new brand.

Reduce costs – Benchmarking against other leading financial institutions indicated that their total occupancy costs were almost 25 per cent higher than the industry average. Representing 20 per cent of their total operating expenses, this was seen as a key area to drive down costs.

Encourage interaction – In the new way of working, employees were going to get much more individual responsibility. However, to ensure that employees would still see and meet each other, to exchange ideas and experiences, the new office should encourage interaction.

Express the brand – A new way of working was an integral part of the company's rebranding strategy, in which it positioned itself as a highly efficient, no-nonsense company. These 'brand values' were to be reflected in the new office.

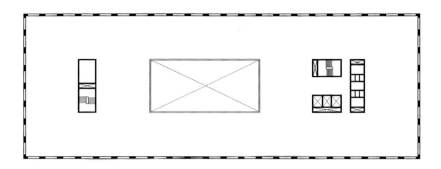

CRUCIAL CHOICES – Before translating these three objectives into a tangible design solution for the refurbishment, various crucial choices were made to change their existing working style.

Location – Although a fully digitalized work process enabled employees to work anywhere at any time, it was decided to keep all employees office-based – not least to guarantee social cohesion and to ensure envisioned levels of interaction.

Use – With almost 50 per cent of the staff working four days a week or fewer and a fully digitalized work process, it was decided to implement desk-sharing for the entire workforce. The circa 1,000 staff were given 800 workstations, leading to significant cost savings.

Layout – Both to encourage interaction and reduce the use of space per workstation, it was decided to keep the work environment as open and transparent as possible.

Appearance – To express the envisioned new brand image, it was decided to keep the 'look and feel' of the office very basic and efficient, while not sacrificing comfort and functionality.

Filing – With the digitalization of the entire business process, there was clearly no room in the office concept for filing cabinets or large personal storage.

Standardization – In line with the desire to be more efficient, the sizes and fit-out of office spaces were fully standardized. Meeting spaces and support spaces, however, were fitted with designer furniture and artwork to stimulate the interaction.

Work spaces	Meeting spaces	Support spaces
Open office (475)	Small meeting room (24x)	Filing space (as needed)
Team space (75x)		Storage space (10x)
Cubicle (250x)		Pantry area (5x)
		Break area (5x)
		Locker area (1,000x)

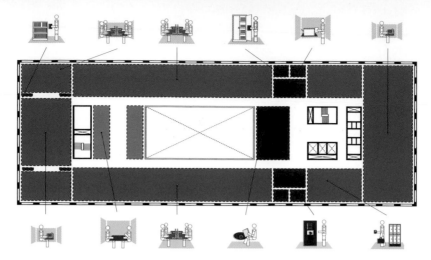

OFFICE SPACES

OFFICE SPACES – In line with the objectives set and choices made, as described above, a variety of office ingredients were selected.

Work spaces – Almost all work spaces were open offices, with the remainder being semi-open cubicles to support activities that require medium concentration and a few team spaces to support collaborative work requiring frequent interaction.

Meeting spaces – As the majority of meetings involved two or three people, six small meeting spaces were implemented per floor. Fitted with flexible partitions, these spaces could be transformed into two large meeting spaces within minutes.

Support spaces – In line with the fully digitalized business process, floors were fitted with very few filing cabinets and only one print and copy area. Furthermore, each floor was fitted with two storage cabinets; one for commonly used office supplies and one for other material, such as corporate brochures and business cards. With the entire workforce sharing desks, sufficient lockers were provided per floor.

ZONING PLAN – Combining the selected office spaces with the available floor plates in the building led to the decision to locate all work spaces along the facade – not least to provide employees access to natural daylight. Subsequently it was decided to locate all meeting spaces in the inner area of the building close to the fire escape and to cluster all support spaces around the main entrance to each floor.

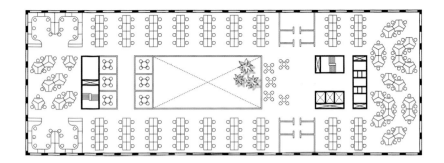

DESIGN SOLUTION – Translating the zoning plan into a tangible fit-out for the back-office of this insurance firm led to the following design solution.

Project summary
- 800 informal workstations over 9,120 square metres (98,170 sq. ft.) total floor area, over four storeys
- 83 per cent work spaces, 6 per cent meeting spaces and 11 per cent support spaces (circulation space excluded)
- 11.4 square metres (123 sq. ft.) per workstation or 9.1 square metres (98 sq. ft.) per employee (including meeting and support spaces)

Attractive cellular office

The merger of three existing research and development units and the aspiration to become one of the leading centres in its field led to the decision to develop a brand new six-storey building with 6,840 square metres (73,630 sq. ft.) for 200 staff. Aiming to attract world-class researchers, an inspiring cellular work environment was created.

Integrating three different units, while avoiding dull or 'dead' office space, the new work environment also needed to support a new organizational culture. Anticipating 10 to 15 per cent growth over the next five years it was decided to realize at least 230 workstations.

Contextual facts
* Research and development centre
* Office with 200 researchers
* Merger of three existing units
* New built six-storey building

OBJECTIVES – To support and enhance the merger of the three groups, it was decided to locate all staff in a new building, ending the leases on the three office buildings where the separate groups had been located. Two objectives were seen as key in achieving their mission: creating an attractive work environment and supporting cultural change.

Attracting and retaining staff – With the aspiration to become a world-class research and development centre, it was seen as key to create an appealing work environment in order to attract and retain highly-skilled and motivated staff. With some of the best researchers greatly valuing privacy and personal space, it was decided mainly to realize private and shared offices in a comfortable and inspiring atmosphere. Also, state-of-the-art technology and high-quality studying facilities were to be implemented.

Supporting cultural change – With the merger of the three different groups, one of the main challenges was to create a new common culture. The envisioned culture was to be dynamic, lively and vivid, creating a place buzzing with ideas and innovations, rather than the conventional work environment associated with 'stuffy' research.

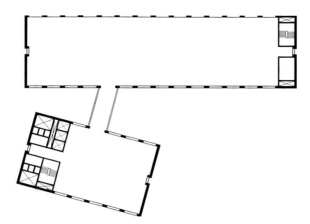

CRUCIAL CHOICES – While translating these two objectives into a physical design solution for the new building, the crucial choices were pretty straightforward.

Location – As most researchers were used to high levels of autonomy in their work, they were free to work at home if they wished to do so. In practice, however, employees were encouraged to work at the office to ensure that they frequently saw each other and did not work in isolation.

Use – With almost every researcher working full-time, spending at least 70 per cent of their time at their computers and very little time in formal meetings, it was decided to give all 200 researchers their own desk.

Layout – To optimally support both concentration activities and collaborative research activities in small groups, it was decided to realize a relatively concealed work environment. Providing privacy and personal space would also help to attract and retain the best researchers.

Appearance – In line with the nature of the work, the image was to be rather casual, somewhat resembling the look and feel of a university, albeit of a higher quality and with better facilities. Furthermore, special attention was given to overview and clear sightlines, avoiding the isolated and non-communicative feel of traditional research offices.

Filing – Although all the researchers worked with advanced technology to access on-line journals and reference works, they still showed a great fondness for papers and books. Therefore the working environment was fitted with sufficient amounts of filing and storage space.

Standardization – Although staff turnover and internal rotations were relatively low, it was decided to fit the building with uniform work spaces and standardized furniture, underlining the egalitarian nature of the organization.

Work spaces	Meeting spaces	Support spaces
Private office (50x)	Large open meeting space (5x)	Filing space (120x)
Shared office (140x)	Small open meeting space (5x)	Storage space (5x)
Team room (40x)		Print and copy area (5x)
		Mail area (5x)
		Pantry area (5x)
		Library (5x)

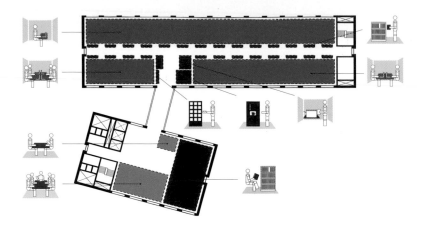

OFFICE SPACES – Following the objectives set and choices made, as outlined above, a variety of office ingredients were selected.

Work spaces – Optimally supporting both concentration activities and collaborative research activities in small groups, all work spaces were enclosed. With 140 shared offices, 50 private offices and 40 team rooms, the total added up to 230 allocated work spaces, anticipating 15 per cent organic growth over the next few years.

Meeting spaces – With few formal meetings, and many short informal meetings of five or more people taking place, each floor was fitted with one large open meeting space. In addition, each floor was fitted with a small open meeting space to support short informal conversations between two to four people.

Support spaces – To store the relatively large amount of working papers and books, each workstation was provided with a filing cabinet. Another decision was to fit each floor with an attractive reading and studying room where people could work when they wanted to 'break away' from their desk.

ZONING PLAN – With the decision to accommodate the organization into a brand-new building, it was relatively easy to translate the envisioned work environment into a zoning plan. It was decided to locate all work spaces along the facade of the main wing, with the meeting spaces and most support spaces in the entrance tower.

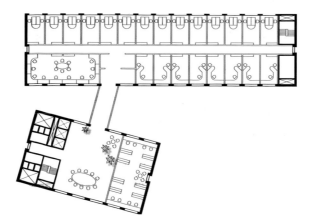

DESIGN SOLUTION – Translating the zoning plan into a concrete fit-out, to accommodate the staff of the newly-formed research and development centre, led to the following design solution.

Project summary

- 230 allocated workstations over 6,840 square metres (73,630 sq. ft.) total floor area, over six storeys
- 67 per cent work spaces, 22 per cent meeting spaces and 11 per cent support spaces (circulation space excluded)
- 29.7 square metres (320 sq. ft.) per workstation or 34.2 square metres (368 sq. ft.) per FTE (including meeting and support spaces)

Creative combination office

With the lease up for renewal, this successful media company with 80 staff decided to leave their existing building and move to a more inspiring work environment. Anticipating further growth, it was decided to relocate to the fourth floor of an historic warehouse, comprising 1,640 square metres (17,650 sq. ft.), that could potentially accommodate up to 100 employees. Aiming to enhance brand identity, a creative combination office was realized.

The company had grown rapidly since its founding almost a decade ago, and the focus could now be redirected from growth alone to enhancing its reputation as being creative and innovative. It was decided to invest in an attractive environment that really matched employee needs and to exploit fully the corporate identity of the company.

Contextual facts
- Medium-sized media company
- Headquarters office with 80 employees
- Relocation due to growth
- Floor in 18th-century warehouse

OBJECTIVES – With the end of the lease period in sight it was time to move away from their current mainstream office space to a more spacious and unique working environment. Driven by the nature of the business, two objectives were set for relocation: optimally supporting creativity and clear brand expression.

Stimulating creativity – With creativity being an essential ingredient of everyday working practices in this media company, it was no surprise that the working environment had to optimally stimulate creativity. Supporting a combination of frequent interaction and focused concentration, it was decided to realize an atelier-like setting with both open and enclosed work spaces.

Expressing the brand – Being based in an overcrowded cellular office for the last few years was not in line with the desired brand image of this media company. The relocation to this 18th-century warehouse was therefore seen not only as a functional necessity, but also as an opportunity to create a 'showcase', where clients, potential staff and other stakeholders would be immersed in the company brand. The implicit wish of management was get free publicity in a variety of media, using the new building as an advertisement for who they were.

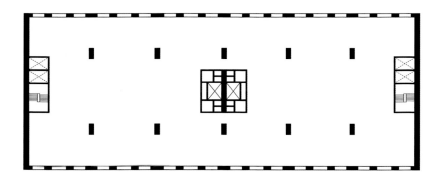

CRUCIAL CHOICES – Before translating these two objectives into a tangible design solution for the relocation, the following crucial choices were made.

Location – With a highly mobile workforce that spends a lot of time at clients' premises, it was decided that employees could work anywhere, any time. However, the new office should be attractive enough to entice employees to work there rather than elsewhere.

Use – Because of the mobile working style and the desire to increase cross-fertilization between employees, it was decided to implement desk-sharing for all non-executive staff. A reasonably fair overcapacity of workplaces should not only prevent queuing but also allow for anticipated future growth.

Layout – To support optimally both communication and concentration activities, it was decided to realize a balanced mix of relatively transparent workstations and relatively concealed workstations.

Appearance – Emphasizing an informal culture, it was decided to realize a playful working environment, with designer furniture and even a brainstorming room. It was believed that this would also significantly enhance the aspired levels of creativity.

Filing – Although most employees were familiar with digital working, there was also a need for sufficient filing and storage space to store not only files and documents, but also specialized equipment needed for daily working practices.

Standardization – Matching the nature of the business and helping to stimulate creativity, a wide variety of furniture was used. In order to meet the needs of mobile workers, however, all furniture was easy to adjust to personal preferences.

Work spaces	Meeting spaces	Support spaces
Open office (64x)	Medium meeting space (2x)	Filing space (24x)
Shared office (16x)	Large meeting room (1x)	Storage space (6x)
Study booth (8x)	Brainstorming room (1x)	Print and copy area (2x)
		Pantry area (2x)
		Break area (1x)
		Waiting area (1x)

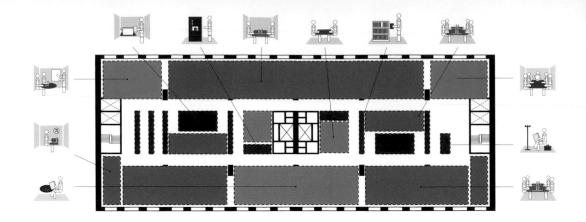

OFFICE SPACES – In line with the objectives set and choices made, as described above, a variety of office ingredients were selected.

Work spaces – Supporting a wide variety of activities, it was decided to implement a generous mix of 64 open offices and 16 shared offices, supported by eight study booths. This would optimally support the highly mobile work, as well as the partners and expert consultants, while allowing for a further ten per cent growth.

Meeting spaces – With most internal meetings comprising three to five employees, two medium meeting spaces were implemented, alongside a large meeting room and a brainstorming room for both internal meetings and larger client meetings. The latter was provided with a flexible partition that allowed multiple small meetings to take place at the same time.

Support spaces – Although digital working was promoted, the new office was fitted with a reasonable amount of filing and storage cabinets – not least because special equipment was needed for daily working practices. Furthermore, a rather generous break area was realized, as well as a small waiting area near the reception desk.

ZONING PLAN – Making best use of the relatively deep floor plan, it was decided to locate most work spaces along the facade and all support spaces in the inner area of the floor. The large meeting room and a brainstorming room were located adjacent to both floor entrances, where clients and employees enter the building, while the medium meeting spaces for internal use were located in the inner area of the building. The break area was located along the facade, right in the middle of the floor plate, functioning as the social heart of the organization.

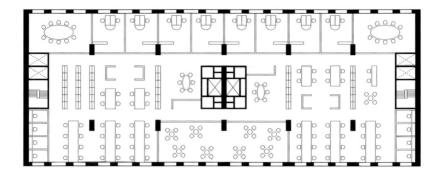

DESIGN SOLUTION – Translating the zoning plan into a tangible fit-out for this medium-sized media company led to the following design solution.

Project summary

- 72 informal and 16 allocated workstations over 1,640 square metres (17,650 sq. ft.) total floor area on one floor
- 60 per cent work spaces, 30 per cent meeting spaces and 10 per cent support spaces (circulation space excluded)
- 18.6 square metres (200 sq. ft.) per workstation or 20.5 square metres (221 sq. ft.) per employee (including meeting and support spaces)

Vibrant club office

Fully embracing a networked way of working, three small consultancy organizations, comprising almost 30 employees, decided to move from their cramped incubator building to a so-called 'club' environment. In order to move closer to the buzz of the city, while having the freedom to creating a unique work environment, they chose to refurbish a 600-square-metre (6,460-sq.-ft.) unit in a city centre period building.

Sharing all facilities with up to 20 freelancers, it was decided to create a 'footloose' environment where clients would be happy to be welcomed.

Contextual facts
* Three small consultancies
* Client-facing for 50 employees
* Relocation and refurbishment
* Unit in city centre period building

OBJECTIVES – The cramped incubator building, where all three companies started and first met, obstructed new ways of working and was not representing the companies enough to the envisioned clientele. Moreover, the cellular structure of the building significantly hindered the exchange of ideas and knowledge that they were aiming for. Overcoming these obstacles, three objectives were selected for their accommodation strategy: encouraging interaction, stimulating creativity and reducing environmental impact.

Encouraging interaction – With communication seen as crucial to social cohesion and cross-fertilization between both the three consultancy firms and the 20 freelancers, interaction needed to be encouraged in every possible way. Subsequently, the refurbishment of their period building should result in an open and transparent work environment with limited to no physical and cultural barriers.

Stimulating creativity – With creativity regarded as key to continuous innovation, chance encounters for enhanced cross-fertilization had to be facilitated where possible. In order to do so, it was decided to realize a club-like setting, with work lounges and a games room, and to pay special attention to the routing within the office.

Reducing environmental impact – Contributing to a greener society, a naturally ventilated building was chosen to reduce energy consumption. To reduce travel-related carbon emissions, it was decided to locate the office near various forms of public transport and to allow for a high degree of homeworking.

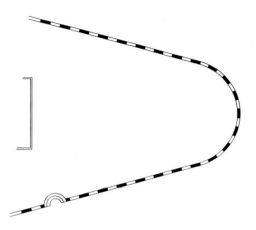

CRUCIAL CHOICES – While translating these three objectives into a physical design solution for the refurbishment, various crucial choices were made to embrace fully new ways of working.

Location – With most employees already accustomed to mobile working, it was decided to create a fully flexible and 'footloose' work environment, where employees could work where and whenever they wanted.

Use – With most employees spending a great deal of time away from the office and a fully wireless IT infrastructure, it was decided to implement desk-sharing for the entire workforce. The circa 30 staff and 20 freelancers were given 44 shared workstations, leading to cost savings and reduced carbon emissions.

Layout – To encourage collaboration, it was decided to keep the work environment as open and transparent as possible, creating a lively buzz at the office. Staff did not regard this as a problem as they were already used to working anywhere, using the office primarily as a meeting place.

Appearance – Despite the highly informal nature of this networking organization, it was decided to create a semi-informal image during refurbishment. It was believed that a somewhat more serious image would signify to their envisioned clientele that they were a mature collective of companies.

Filing – In line with new ways of working and supporting shared use of all workstations, a fully paperless work environment was aspired to. Also, reduced paper use and the lack of filing cabinets would have a positive impact on the environment.

Standardization – With a fully flexible work environment with shared use of workstations, it was straightforward to fit the refurbished building with standardized furniture only. In order to stimulate creativity, however, the different areas within the unit were fitted with furniture from different designers.

Work spaces	Meeting spaces	Support spaces
Open office (22x)	Medium meeting room (2x)	Print and copy area (1x)
Work lounge (10x)	Small meeting space (2x)	Mail area (1x)
Touch down (12x)	Meeting point (1x)	Pantry area (1x)
		Locker area (1x)
		Games room (1x)

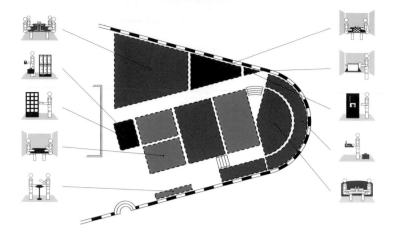

OFFICE SPACES – Following the objectives set and choices made, as outlined above, a variety of office ingredients were selected.

Work spaces – To encourage interaction while stimulating creativity, nearly all work spaces were open. With 22 open offices, ten work lounges and 12 touch downs, the total added up to 44 shared work spaces.

Meeting spaces – With a fair number of client meetings to allow for, two medium meeting rooms were located next to each other and fitted with a flexible partition. Furthermore, two small meeting spaces were realized in the club area, with a meeting point near the entrance of the building.

Support spaces – In line with the aspiration to create a paperless office, a very limited amount of space for filing and storage was combined with the locker area and the mail area. Furthermore, the print and pantry areas were combined to form a one-stop service point. In addition, a games room was provided as a reminder of their early days and to accommodate the highly popular and competitive pool games that were being held between the three companies.

ZONING PLAN – Combining the selected office ingredients with the selected office unit led to the decision to locate most work spaces along the facade. The work lounges and small meeting spaces were located in the deliberately lowered centre of the unit to create a club-like atmosphere. The meeting rooms and the combined locker and mail area were located in the inner area of the unit, but close to the main entrance.

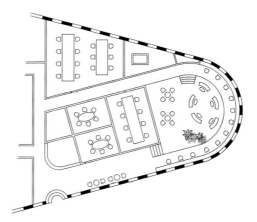

DESIGN SOLUTION – Translating the zoning plan into a concrete fit-out to accommodate 50 employees in a networked club environment, led to the following design solution.

Project summary

- 44 informal workstations over 600 square metres (6,460 sq. ft.) total floor area in one unit
- 63 per cent work spaces, 25 per cent meeting spaces and 13 per cent support spaces (circulation space excluded)
- 13.6 square metres (146 sq. ft.) per workstation or 12 square metres (129 sq. ft.) per worker (including meeting and support spaces)

As new office concepts tend to encounter resistance, proactively involving employees during implementation is highly recommended

Client Parliament
Location Portland, United States
Design Chris Erickson

IMPLEMENTATION

Whereas all previous chapters focused on the tangible ingredients necessary to develop a new office concept, this chapter focuses on the equally important implementation process. Although a proposed office concept may very well be the most appropriate solution for a specific organization, many projects do not reach their full potential due to a badly managed implementation process.

The main challenge when implementing a new office concept is that it will generally encounter resistance, as some employees will perceive change as a threat. However, resistance can be reduced, and sometimes even turned into acceptance, by carefully and proactively implementing and developing the new concept. Among other things, this means engaging, informing and involving end-users and making a careful analysis of the actual needs of the organization. In addition, successful implementation even asks for a certain degree of strong headedness, dedication and passion for the envisioned change.

The following pages provide six recommendations for successful implementation of new office concepts:

* Analyze
* Communicate
* Involve
* Integrate
* Care and preserve
* Be brave

Analyze

As this publication intends to show, there is an overwhelming number of possibilities in office design. There are few absolutes and every organization is unique in its needs and ambitions. For example, the perfect environment for a design studio would not work for a law firm and vice versa. Therefore, the first step in developing an office concept is making a thorough analysis of the organization that has to be accommodated.

When analyzing the organization, aspects that have to be looked at are: strategy, structure, work processes and culture. The analysis should pay attention to both the current situation ('as is') and the desired future situation ('to be'). The 'as is' situation can be studied by observing everyday work processes on the work floor. The 'to be' situation can be analyzed by talking to management and looking at general trends in society and technology. Please note: a common mistake is to focus one-sidedly on a desirable and visionary 'to be' situation, while ignoring the messiness of everyday practice.

There are several tools available for analyzing organizations and their accommodation needs. Well-known are quantitative tools, such as 'space utilization studies', that make a detailed analysis of how spaces are used over time, or 'workplace surveys' in which employees are asked about their working patterns. Both tools provide 'hard' data, which provide a solid basis for design. It is important to acknowledge, however, that they miss out on 'softer' organizational issues, such as the degree of trust or the importance of status symbols within an organization. To get a grip on such intangible but critical aspects, qualitative tools such as interviews can be used, in combination with a trained eye for office culture.

Frequently used tools
- On-line employee surveys
- Space utilization studies
- Interviews with employees
- Observation studies
- Scenario analysis of future developments

Relevant considerations
- Are there enough time and resources available for analysis and research?
- Should the analysis be done by an 'insider' (more inside knowledge, less expensive), or an 'outsider' (a fresh look, more expertise)?
- Have employees been informed about why, for example, space utilization studies are taking place? Will it raise certain expectations that need to be 'managed'?
- Do questions in interviews and surveys provide room for 'strategic' answering (e.g. to oppose certain office concepts)?

Communicate

To create awareness and harness engagement among employees, clear communication from the start of a project is essential. The future users of a new office concept should know why, when and how their work environment will change. This helps to avoid confusion and/or misleading expectations.

For starters, employees should be informed about the need and the objectives for a new office concept. What is it that the new concept should achieve: cost reduction, cultural change, enhanced interaction, staff morale, etc.? Such issues are best explained by top management, stipulating the overall course for the project. Later in the process, communication should focus more on what the office concept will look like and how it will work in daily practice.

In all communication, it is important to be constructive and to underline the positive aspects of the new office concept (e.g. more freedom in time and place of working, greater choice of types of work space, better information and communication technology). At the same time, however, it is important to be honest and open about the potential downsides of cost-driven decisions (e.g. no more private offices, or less space per employee).

To keep employees engaged during the whole project, a steady stream of information and communication should be maintained. Especially during the design process, there will be plenty of opportunities to communicate about the envisioned new work environment, using computer animations, artist impressions and real-life mock-ups. Next to that, it is important to communicate about more mundane issues such as clean desk policies or the new computer system.

Frequently used tools
- Presentations (e.g. by management or the architect/consultant)
- Newsletters
- Intranet (e.g. a dedicated project website)
- Mock-ups
- Exhibitions with drawings/models of the new office
- Instruction books with practical guidelines for using the new office

Relevant considerations
- Is there a communication department that can help to set up the communication strategy?
- Which players in the process are most convincing, well respected or with enough authority to communicate about the office to the organization (e.g. top management, project champions, the interior designer)?
- Is the communication clear and accessible enough to be heard by employees?
- Is communication one-way or will future users have the ability to comment on and criticize the new plans?

Involve

Office design is not an autonomous process that should be driven by experts only. Involving end-users in the process ensures that solutions will be usable and meet the needs of the organization. A crucial side effect of user involvement is that users are likely to see the concept as 'theirs' when they have been involved in the development process.

The main question is to what extent users should be involved in the project. Participation can range from 'co-thinking' to 'co-decision making' and even 'co-creation'. Generally speaking, high levels of user involvement lead to high levels of acceptance. Potential risks, however, are that employees will be reasoning beyond their expertise and that they use their involvement to prevent change. If not well managed, user participation may result in endless discussions and compromise solutions that satisfy almost no one.

The art of participation is to let office design flourish within set boundaries. In advance, management should determine the scope and limitations of involvement. As on other topics, management should take several strategic decisions (see 'critical choices' chapter), which can then be worked out in cooperation with end-users. But this only makes sense when user involvement is taken seriously; otherwise it will result in a loss of trust, which will hamper the project's success.

Frequently used tools
- Workshops and brainstorming sessions
- The creation of 'focus groups' that review design solutions
- The creation of 'work groups' that work on particular user-topics (e.g. gathering data on the need for filing space or the number of meeting spaces)
- Excursions with users to other projects (to provide them with inspiration and alternative insights)
- Formal representation of users in the steering committee

Relevant considerations
- Does the involved user group consist of the right mix of people (interested, critical, open to change, coming from different levels and departments)?
- On what topics will users be able to provide input (e.g. the overall concept, the detailed design, the choice of furniture)?
- Is the design team open to and used to working with end-users?
- Will the involvement of users possibly obstruct or clash with the objectives that management has set for the project?
- Will employees receive serious feedback on how their input has been incorporated into the design?
- Is there a risk that the design process will become an arena for discussions about issues other than the physical workplace (e.g. frustrations about reorganizations or management styles)?
- Does an organization already have a formalized way of involving employees in decision making (e.g. by means of a Workers' Council)?

Integrate

The development and implementation of a new office concept generally involves more than the physical work environment alone. It also entails the way of working, the style of management, the use of information technology and potentially a revised organizational culture.

Because of the integral nature of workplace change, the project should integrate expertise from the organization's HR department and IT department, and also from the departments that deal with marketing and communication. The HR department will be able to see whether the new work environment can be aligned with existing change programmes. Similarly, the IT department is often best placed to advise on IT solutions, which are critical when introducing more mobile and flexible office concepts. In addition, the marketing department will be able to help the design team to specify how the office environment can help to build and 'live' the organization's brand.

In short, it is highly recommended to take an integral approach when developing and implementing a new work environment. Do not just take a facilities management or design approach, but integrate the different physical, social and virtual aspects of the work environment into one single and coherent workplace strategy.

Frequently used tools
* Mapping organizational change programmes (in HR, IT and/or marketing)
* The creation of specific work groups for IT and/ or HR topics
* Involvement of HR, IT and marketing experts in the project team
* Presentations by HR, IT and marketing experts on changes in their field to inform and discuss with other user groups and the project team.

Relevant considerations
* What type of organizational changes does the new work environment require in order to be successful (e.g. technology for digital filing, cultural change, new management styles)?
* How difficult or easy will it be to implement these changes (e.g. cultural change is notoriously difficult)?
* Is there a need to accelerate or even push particular changes?
* Which other change programmes are taking place within the organization and how can they be aligned or supported with the new office concept?
* How cooperative and open to change are the HR, IT and marketing departments? Will they strengthen or slow the desired changes?
* Do the departments in question have sufficient expertise and knowledge of current developments to help the project, or is there a need for external expertise?

Care and preserve

New office concepts have to be looked after once they have been created. When moving in, it is important to take care of possible 'teething' troubles, as nothing is perfect first time around. To do so, provide a central point where employees can post complaints and/or suggestions for improvement. Furthermore, the new concept should ideally be evaluated after several months in use to make further improvements.

It is important to keep a close watch on how people behave in the new office. All too often employees will relapse to their old behaviour. Especially in flexible office concepts this can be a problem. Think of managers 'squatting' in meeting rooms, using them as their private offices, or people marking their personal territory with piles of paper and personal belongings. To avoid such problems, certain rules should be set (and adhered to), without being overly strict or patronizing. Think of protocols for homeworking, clean desking, the use of shared spaces and dealing with distracting activities such as telephoning in open office spaces.

The role of management is critical in preserving the concept successfully. Rules and instruction books make little sense if managers don't set an example. They are the ones that should play an exemplary role and explain why and how the concept should be used. At a certain point, however, the new behaviour should come naturally and not require too much 'policing'. If a concept really needs to be enforced in its everyday usage, it is probably not the right concept.

Frequently used tools
- A 'mailbox' for complaints and/or suggestions
- Post-occupancy evaluation surveys
- Daily check on clean desking (when relevant)
- Instruction books with practical guidelines for using the new office

Relevant considerations
- Is there adequate follow-up on complaints and suggestions as well as comments and questions? Is the follow-up clearly communicated?
- How representative are the filed complaints? Do they come from the five per cent critical minority or the large majority of users?
- Are problems of a physical nature (e.g. printers that do not work properly) or more of an organizational nature (e.g. managers finding it difficult to manage mobile employees)?
- Are problems 'real' or more a matter of 'getting used to it'? (Please note: either way they have to be taken seriously.)

Be brave

It is not easy to change and improve the office environment. Just like any other change, it is likely to raise resistance among employees. Sometimes this resistance indicates serious weaknesses in the concept, other times people are just wary of new ideas. Either way, resistance has to be taken seriously and taken into account in the implementation process.

The previous sections in this chapter gave several basic guidelines for dealing with resistance. Next to all that, however, creating a new office concept also calls for bravery, dedication and belief in the envisioned change. To a certain extent, changes have to be pushed ahead. Giving in to everybody's wishes and trying to please all stakeholders tends to result in watered-down solutions that do not work. It is important to know that when a (well designed) office concept is finally realized and people are working in it, resistance tends to die out quickly (apart from the ever-present five per cent of sceptical employees).

So, change also asks for leadership, and it is management that should take this role. Critical changes that affect everyday work life and employee performance should not be considered as an issue only for facility managers or outside consultants or designers. Office design is a management issue that requires several strategic decisions from management, concerning space, place and processes. The details can then be filled in, using the expertise from different disciplines, users and the design team.

Frequently used tools
* Bravery, dedication and belief in the new office concept

Relevant considerations
* Is resistance induced by 'irrational' fear of change or by serious weaknesses in the concept?
* Is management capable and committed enough to drive the change process?
* Will management and the design team act convincingly and persuasively when they encounter resistance?
* What are the topics on which resistance is expected and how can that be dealt with?
* Is the resistance related to the office concept, or is the office concept a focal point for frustrations concerning other organizational or management issues?

This chapter provides an overview of relevant books, journals and magazines as well as research centres and professional institutions

Client Spaces
Location Amsterdam, the Netherlands
Design Sevil Peach

FURTHER INFORMATION

For readers seeking more information about workplace and office design, this chapter sums up the most relevant books, journals and magazines. It also provides an overview of leading research centres and professional institutions committed to generating more knowledge in this field.

Books and publications

Allen, T., A. Bell, R. Graham, B. Hardy and F. Swaffer (2004), **Working Without Walls**, London: Crown.

In this renowned government publication, the authors celebrate some of the best workplace projects taking place within the UK government. The book analyzes historical context and the catalysts for change, highlights emerging best practice and summarizes lessons learnt.

Allen, T.J. and G.W. Henn (2007), **The Organization and Architecture of Innovation: managing the flow of technology**, Oxford: Butterworth-Heinemann.

Thomas Allen and Gunter Henn explore the combined use of two management tools to make the innovation process most effective: organizational structure and physical space. They highlight how these tools can transform organizations to maximize the 'communication for inspiration' that is central to the innovation process.

Becker, F. (2004), **Offices at Work: uncommon work space strategies that add value and improve performance**, San Francisco: Jossey-Bass.

In this highly accessible book, leading workplace thinker Franklin Becker explains fundamental design issues for managers and executives. He provides a broad range of insights and practical explanations of how different 'uncommon' solutions work and make sense, using real world examples.

Blyth, A. and J. Worthington (2010), **Managing the Brief for Better Design**, London: E&FN Spon.

In this new and updated edition of their essential book on briefing, Alastair Blyth and John Worthington offer an understanding of the briefing process and its importance to the built environment. Through better briefing, clients will be able to make building-related decisions with greater confidence.

Botton, A. de (2009), **The Pleasures and Sorrows of Work**, London: Hamish Hamilton.

In this illuminating book, philosopher Alain de Botton provides vivid portraits of a range of occupations, generating a good deal of useful discussion about contemporary work life. For all those involved in office design, the chapter about an accountant is highly interesting – is this what office life should be like, or rather the opposite?

Clements-Croome, D. (2000), **Creating the Productive Workplace**, London: E & FN Spon.

This comprehensive book provides a critical and multidisciplinary review of the relationship between productivity and the work environment. Through an international group of experts, important factors affecting workplace productivity are set out and practical solutions for a productive work environment are provided.

Duffy, F. (2008), **Work and the City**, London: Black Dog Publishing.

In this condensed, challenging publication, Francis Duffy reflects on the changing nature of work in an urban context, providing an excellent overview of both the evolution of cities and knowledge workplaces, and their possible futures.

Duffy, F. (1997), **The New Office**, London: Conran Octopus.

This book is a classic, in which Francis Duffy explores the legacy and lessons of a century of office design and looks at how information technology has transformed the way we work, including the environments we work in.

Eisele, J., C. Volm and B. Staniek (2005), **Bürobau Atlas: grundlagen, planung, technologie, arbeitsplatzqualitäten**, München: Callwey.

A real and comprehensive atlas on office design, the authors cover a wide range of office design topics – from workplace design and indoor climate to the impact of colours. Branded as the 'Neufert for office design', this book is unfortunately only available in German.

Florida, R. (2007), **The Rise of the Creative Class: and how it's transforming work, leisure, community and everyday life**, New York: Basic Books.

In this international bestseller, Richard Florida highlights the increased importance of creativity in all types of organizations and in the wider society in general. He chronicles the ongoing sea change in people's choices and attitudes, and shows not only what's happening but also how it stems from a fundamental economic change. Interestingly, he dedicates a special chapter to the relation between workplace design and creativity.

Gall, C., and B. Arantes (2009), **Office Code**, Grand Rapids: Steelcase.

Based on extensive research, Catherine Gall and Beatriz Arantes show how workers from different countries think differently about work and workplaces. The book spans six European countries – the United Kingdom, the Netherlands, Germany, France, Italy and Spain – explaining and describing a wide diversity of office cultures.

Grech, C., and D. Walters (2008), **The Future Office: design, practice and applied research**, New York: Taylor & Francis.

Edited by Christopher Grech and David Walters, this book examines the implications of the IT revolution and the resulting knowledge-based economy on current urban design and identifies potential new trends in office design from an international perspective.

Hardy, B., R. Graham, P. Stansall, A. White, A. Harrison, A. Bell and L. Hutton (2008), **Working Beyond Walls**, London: Crown.

Following on from *Working Without Walls*, the authors explore the role of the workplace as an agent for change and describe a vision for government workplaces of the future.

Horgen, T.H., M.L. Joroff, W.L. Porter and D.A. Schön (1998), **Excellence by Design: bridging the boundaries of work, process and space**, New York: John Wiley & Sons.

A book from the 'last century' that hasn't lost any of its relevance. Based on extensive research, the authors explore how the workplace interacts with work practices, introducing the 'process architecture' approach to creating workplaces.

Jensen, P.A. (2009), **Facilities Management for Students and Practitioners**, Copenhagen: Centre for Facilities Management – Realdania Research.

In this accessible book, Per Anker Jensen offers a coherent and comprehensive introduction to the relatively new professional discipline called Facilities Management. Used by both practitioners and students, he explicitly pays attention to the design and management of office work spaces.

Kampschroer, K., K.M. Powell, K. Kelly and J. Heerwagen (2006), **Workplace Matters**, Washington: General Services Administration.

In this practical publication, the authors argue that the emphasis of workplace design should be on the people and the work they accomplish. Through a structured approach and applied measures, they show clear links between physical infrastructure and organizational performance

Knittel-Ammerschuber, S. (2006), **Architecture: the Element of Success – building strategies and business objectives**, Basel: Birkhäuser.

In this well-designed book, the author argues that communication, transparency, flexibility and openness are key values to successful businesses, which must be reflected in a company's architecture.

Marmot, A.F., and J. Eley (2000), **Office Space Planning: designs for tomorrow's workplace**, New York: McGraw-Hill.

Another classic, in which Alexi Marmot and Joanna Eley provide practical insights that help clients, interior designers and space planners to design office buildings that meet organizational needs.

Myerson, J., and P. Ross (2006), **Space to Work: new office design**, London: Laurence King Publishing.

In this attractive book, Jeremy Myerson and Philip Ross showcase 40 office projects from around the world. The projects illustrate four emerging 'realms' for knowledge work: the Academy, the Guild, the Agora and the Lodge.

Stegmeier, D. (2008), **Innovations in Office Design: the critical influence approach to effective work environments**, New Jersey: John Wiley & Sons.

Diane Stegmeier offers key lessons on preventing workplace strategy failure. She introduces a practical approach to integrating cultural, operational and environmental organizational elements fostering desired behaviours to support business goals when designing an office.

Sundström, E. (1986), **Work Places: the psychology of the physical environment in offices and factories**. New York: Cambridge University Press.

One of the first and best books on how physical surroundings affect people who work in offices (and factories). Sundström discusses topics such as individual satisfaction and performance, interpersonal relationships and group cohesion, as well as organizational effectiveness.

Van der Voordt, D.J.M. (2003), **Cost and Benefits of Innovative Workplace Design**, Delft: Center for People and Buildings.

Based on an extensive literature review and his own research data, Theo van der Voordt provides one of the best overviews of evidence on how office concepts affect employee satisfaction, productivity and occupancy costs.

Van Meel, J.J. (2000), **The European Office**, Rotterdam: 010 Publishers.

This book shows how standards in office architecture and workplace design differ strongly from country to country. It explains how form does not only follow function, but also local business culture, regulations, market conditions and the urban context.

Van Ree, H.J. (2008), **IPD Space Code: measuring the space performance of buildings**, London: IPD Occupiers.

This publication provides a good practice framework for measuring, analyzing and reporting on space use and subsequent performance. Furthermore, it provides valuable insights on optimizing space usage.

Worthington, J. (2005), **Reinventing the Workplace**, Oxford: Architectural Press.

Edited by John Worthington, this book contains a series of essays that provide ideas, inspiration and analysis of the multitude of ways in which a work environment can be designed and managed.

Journals and magazines

Building Research & Information – International refereed scientific journal focusing on buildings and their supporting systems. www.tandf.co.uk

Dezeen – Popular on-line magazine that features state-of-the-art architecture, design and interiors projects from around the world. www.dezeen.com

Facilities – Peer-reviewed scientific journal covering the multidisciplinary topics of people, property and process management in relation to the workplace. www.emeraldinsight.com

Facilities Management Journal – Practical, UK-oriented magazine targeted at facility managers. www.fmj.co.uk

FM World – Magazine by BIFM carrying industry news, case studies and interviews on facilities management. www.bifm.org.uk

Mensch & Büro – German magazine dealing with design and business issues. www.menschundbuero.de

Office et Culture – French trend magazine on office environments that aims to help its readers bring greater efficiency, health and well-being into the work environment. www.office-et-culture.fr

Onoffice – Stylish on-line magazine that offers insight, criticism and practical knowledge concerning commercial office space. www.onofficemagazine.com

The Leader – Magazine by CoreNet providing current and new thinking on corporate real estate and workplace issues. www.corenetglobal.org

Research centres

Center for People and Buildings
Delft University of Technology
Delft, the Netherlands
www.cfpb.nl

The Center for People and Buildings is an independent knowledge centre that focuses on the interrelations between people, work and workplaces. Its mission is to stimulate research, product development and knowledge transfer within the fields of real estate and facilities management.

Centre for Facilities Management – Realdania Research
Denmark Technical University
Copenhagen, Denmark
www.cfm.dtu.dk

The Centre for Facilities Management is a Danish national research centre established to strengthen research on facilities management. To fulfil its mission, research is directed at dealing with designing, developing and operating buildings and infrastructure so that they are constantly adjusted to user needs.

CEM Facility Services Research
Helsinki University of Technology
Helsinki, Finland
www.cem.tkk.fi/fsr

CEM Facility Services Research is a research group that specializes in the construction and facility services businesses. The group produces scientific research results to meet the needs of the Finnish construction and facility services industries, but has a strong international focus.

Center for Building Performance and Diagnostics
Carnegie Mellon University
Pittsburgh, Pennsylvania
www.cmu.edu

The Center for Building Performance and Diagnostics at Carnegie Mellon University works hand in hand with members of the Advanced Building Systems Integration Consortium to establish research, demonstration and policy activities for the Consortium. Their main focus is on building services, indoor climate and technology.

Centre for Facilities Management Development
Sheffield Hallam University
Sheffield, United Kingdom
www.shu.ac.uk

As a part of the Sheffield Business School, the Centre for Facilities Management Development primarily carries out academic, grant-aided and contract-based research, to deliver leading-edge education and training and offer consultancy services in all aspects of facilities management.

Centre for Real Estate and Facilities Management
Norwegian Institute for Science and Technology
Trontheim, Norway
www.metamorfose.ntnu.no

The Centre for Real Estate and Facilities Management provides high-quality education and information on the strategic value of real estate and facilities management. This is done in collaboration with other research centres, real estate owners and facilities managers as well as developers, contractors and end-users.

CRC for Construction Innovation
Queensland University of Technology
Brisbane, Australia
www.construction-innovation.info

The Cooperative Research Centre for Construction Innovation is an Australian research, development and implementation centre focused on the needs of the property, design, construction and facility management sectors.

Helen Hamlyn Centre
Royal College of Art
London, UK
www.hhc.rca.ac.uk

The Helen Hamlyn Centre at the Royal College of Art in London takes a people-centred approach to innovation and workplace design. Its multidisciplinary team of experts recently performed interesting research on how the physical work environment should respond to the needs and requirements of an ageing working population.

International Workspace Studies Program
Cornell University, USA
http://iwsp.human.cornell.edu

The International Workspace Studies Program (IWSP) at Cornell University explores how innovative workplace strategies and the ecology of new ways of working can enhance the triple bottom-line. Research efforts are split into three separate but related areas: the Corporate Workplace, Healing Environments and Sustainable Planning & Design.

Office Innovation Center
Fraunhofer-Institute
Stuttgart, Germany
www.oic.fhg.de

At the Fraunhofer Office Innovation Center the future of work is being researched, lived and demonstrated. Experts from five Fraunhofer Institutes work out prototypical solutions for the office world of tomorrow. The federal government, the government of Baden-Württemberg and numerous enterprises support this project, which is unique in Germany.

Professional institutions

BIFM
www.bifm.org.uk

The British Institute of Facilities Management (BIFM) provides information, education, training and networking services for over 12,000 members – both individual professionals and organizations. The Institute is inclusive, working across related disciplines and forming alliances with like-minded professional bodies. BIFM is a founding member of both EuroFM and GlobalFM.

BOMA
www.boma.org

Building Owners and Managers Association (BOMA) International represents 92 local associations throughout the United States and 13 international affiliates. BOMA focuses on actively and responsibly representing and promoting the interests of the commercial real estate industry.

BCO
www.bco.org.uk

The British Council for Offices' (BCO) mission is to research, develop and communicate best practice in all aspects of the office sector. It delivers this by providing a forum for the discussion and debate of relevant issues. Its members are all organizations involved in creating, acquiring or occupying office space, whether architects, lawyers, surveyors, financial institutions or public agencies.

CABE
www.cabe.org.uk

The Commission for Architecture and the Built Environment (CABE) helps public agencies and advises clients, contractors, architects and planners to create value through better design. They are most famous for their design review service, which helps clients to seize opportunities and avoid mistakes. Furthermore, they promote education, skills and careers for the built environment and conduct research, frequently resulting in publications available from their website.

CIB
www.cibworld.nl

The Conseil International du Bâtiment (CIB) or International Council for Buildings is a global network of over 5,000 experts from about 500 member organizations with a research, university, industry or government background. The network is set up for international exchange and cooperation in research and innovation in building and construction in support of an improved building process and of improved performance of the built environment.

CoreNet
www.corenetglobal.org

The Corporate Real Estate Network (CoreNet) is a global professional association that focuses on corporate real estate end-users and includes in its membership all components of the supply chain that create value for corporate occupiers of real estate. Therefore, CoreNet connects diverse functional disciplines, industries, companies, locations and individuals.

EuroFM
www.eurofm.org

EuroFM is an open network of professionals, academics and researchers, all focused on facilities management. They are based in more than 15 European countries and represent professional associations, education and research institutes and corporate organizations. Its mission is the advancement of knowledge in facilities management in Europe and its application in practice, education and research.

GlobalFM
www.globalfm.org

GlobalFM is a worldwide alliance of member-centred facilities management organizations, such as BIFM, FMA (Facilities Management Australia) and SAFMA (South African Facilities Management Association), which represent professionals involved in the strategic and operational management of facilities for both public and private sector organizations and often organize networking events, trend updates and advisory services.

IFMA
www.ifma.org

The International Facility Management Association (IFMA) is the world's largest and most widely recognized international association for professional facilities managers, supporting more than 19,500 members in 60 countries. IFMA certifies facility managers, conducts research, provides educational programmes, recognizes facilities management certificate programmes and produces World Workplace, the world's largest facilities management conference and exposition.

Client Caballero Fabriek
Location The Hague, the Netherlands
Design GROUP A

About the authors

Juriaan van Meel is a senior consultant at ICOP, a workplace consultancy firm in the Netherlands, which he co-founded. He is also a senior researcher at Centre for Facilities Management – Realdania Research in Copenhagen. His previous publications include *The European Office* and, as co-author, *The Office, the Whole Office and Nothing but the Office*.

Yuri Martens is a researcher and practitioner on workplace strategy, combining his Ph.D. research on creative work environments with strategic workplace consultancy. Previously he worked at the Center for People and Buildings in the Netherlands, where he co-authored *Werkplekwijzer*, the Dutch predecessor of this book.

Hermen Jan van Ree is a senior consultant on strategy, operations and marketing – specializing in performance management. Previously he worked as a senior research fellow at University College London and various research institutes in the Netherlands and the United States. He is an active member of the BIFM and a principal expert to the European Committee for Standardization.

About the reviewers

Francis Duffy is a British architect and a founder of DEGW, the international architectural and design practice best known for office design and workplace strategy. Duffy is particularly noted for his work on the future of the office and the flexible use of space. He is a prolific writer and the author of many books, including *The New Office* and *Work and the City*.

Michael Joroff is a Senior Lecturer at MIT and directed the MIT Laboratory of Architecture and Planning for 18 years. As an international consultant on real estate strategy, Joroff specializes in corporate infrastructure management and organizational workplace design. He is the author of numerous publications, including *Excellence by Design*.

Siri Blakstad is a professor at the centre for Real Estate and Facilities Management – Norwegian University of Science and Technology. Her field of expertise is focused on the planning and operation of space in order to support the user organization and its needs. Her current research aims at developing methods for strategic briefing and workplace design.

Photography credits

Anders Sune Berg 66a, 70a, 84a, 90a **André** 60a, 74b **Bastiaan IngenHousz** 96b **Benjamin Benschneider** 52c **Cesar Rubio** 18, 138 **Chantal Wouters** 76c **Christiaan de Bruyne** 42b, 46c, 56c, 60c, 68c, 84c **David Barbour** 94c **David Wakely** 92a **Dennis Gilbert** 16, 46b, 76a **Edsard Vegter** 74c **Elsje van Ree** 68a **Eric Laignel** 62c, 64c, 90b **Francesco Radino** 38, 44b, 66c, 82a, 88c, 132, 142 **Gerard Vlekke** 78a **H.G. Esch** 2, 40a, 48c, 96c **Hans Morren** 40c, 52b, 74a **Harold Pereira** 50c, 56b, 86a **Hugo Potharst** 68b **Imade Alexander Mul** 80c **Iwan Baan** 10 **Jaani Vaahtera** 6, 50b, 62b **Jacob Nielsen** 30, 50a, 60b, 64a **Jeppe Carlsen** 8 **Jeroen Musch** 48a **Joep Jacobs** 86c **Joerg Hempel** 76b **John Dee** 54b **Joop van Reeken** 70c **Joost van den Broek** 54c, 124, 134 **Jørgen True** 84b, 90c **Josh Dunford** 40b **Kim Zwarts** 80a **Lincoln Barbour** 116, 136 **Luuk Kramer** 54a **MHK Photography** 42a, 82b **Mrigank Sharma** 98 **Nic Lehoux** 12, 44c **Nick Guttridge** 72 **Peter Bliek** 78b, 82c **Peter Wurmli** 48b, 92b **Pieter Boersma** 88b **Renzo Mazzolini** 4, 52a, 56a, 58, 64b, 70b, 94b, 140 **Roos Aldershoff** 66b **Ryan Pyle** 44a **Scagliola Brakkee** 14, 46a, 80b, 86b, 96a, 130 **SHCA** 78c **Søren Kuhn & Jørgen True** 62a, 88a **Svenska Dagbladet** 94a **Vlad Caprarescu** 92c **Yves Paternoster** 42c

Offices should support a range of activities – not just desk work

Client Mother
Location London, United Kingdom
Design Clive Wilkinson Architects

Client Spaces
Location Amsterdam, the Netherlands
Design Sevil Peach

Even in a fully digital world, people need space to get work done

Client Parliament
Location Portland, United States
Design Chris Erickson

Informal meetings
may be best supported
by informal spaces

Efficient open spaces
are not necessarily
noisy or unattractive

Client facebook
Location Palo Alto, United States
Design studio o+a

Face-to-face interaction is crucial for the social life of organizations

Client BBC Scotland
Location Glasgow, United Kingdom
Design Graven Images

New ways
of working
mix well
with old
period
buildings

Client 5+1AA
Location Genoa, Italy
Design 5+1AA

IN ASSOCIATION WITH:

Center for People and Buildings
Kluyverweg 6
2629 HT Delft
The Netherlands
www.cfpb.nl

**Centre for Facilities Management –
Realdania Research**
Technical University of Denmark
Building 424
2800 Lyngby
Denmark
www.cfm.dtu.dk

SPONSORED BY:

ICOP
Schiekade 830
3032 AL Rotterdam
The Netherlands
www.icop.nl

Ahrend
Laarderhoogtweg 12
1101 EA Amsterdam Z.O.
The Netherlands
www.ahrend.com

HUMANISING_SPACES

LAURENCE KING

Published in 2010 by
Laurence King Publishing Ltd
361–373 City Road
London EC1V 1LR
United Kingdom

T: +44 20 7841 6900
F: +44 20 7841 6910
E: enquiries@laurenceking.com
W: www.laurenceking.com

Copyright © 2010 Juriaan van Meel, Yuri Martens,
Hermen Jan van Ree and Center for People and Buildings.
The moral right of the authors has been asserted.

Original Dutch edition published as: Van Meel, J., Y.
Martens, G. Hofkamp, D. Jonker and A. Zeegers (2006),
Werkplekwijzer, Delft: Center for People and Buildings / The
Hague: Dutch Government Buildings Agency.

A catalogue for this book is available from the British Libra·

ISBN: 978 1 85669 698 2

Design: Studio Sander Boon
Iconography: Juriaan van Meel

Printed and bound in China